Joanna Goldsworthy was ... grew up in South and East A... working in London publis... ...editorial consultant and freelance e...or and writer, and is the editor of *A Certain Age: Reflecting on the Menopause.*

MOTHERS

By Daughters

Edited by
Joanna Goldsworthy

A *Virago* Book

First published in Great Britain by VIRAGO PRESS 1995

Reprinted 1995 (three times), 1996

A CIP catalogue record for this book is available
from the British Library

ISBN 1 85381 793 7

Printed in England by Clays Ltd, St Ives plc

UK companies, institutions and other organizations wishing
to make bulk purchases of this or any other books
published by Little, Brown, should contact their local
bookshop or the special sales department at the address below.
Tel 0171 911 8000. Fax 0171 911 8100.

Virago
A Division of
Little, Brown and Company (UK)
Brettenham House
Lancaster Place
London WC2E 7EN

ACKNOWLEDGEMENTS

My thanks to the contributors who have explored their feelings about their relationship with their mothers with such insight, humour and honesty, painful though this has been for them; and to Ruth Petrie for her encouragement and excellent editorial advice.

CONTENTS

INTRODUCTION

Joanna Goldsworthy

Propped against the lamp on my desk is a photograph, taken towards the end of the last century, of a mother and daughter. The mother is young and beautiful, her blonde hair caught into a soft chignon. She looks down at the child on her lap, her expression loving and gentle, but fearful too: that of the willing victim. The daughter, too large to sit comfortably on her mother's knee, is nevertheless intent on staying there, her arm clenched round her mother's neck. Her eyes are locked fiercely on to her parent's, willing her, if she dares, to relax her gaze.

Or could it be that the child's other hand is imprisoned in her mother's grasp, that her bare legs are tensed for escape, that she is obliged against her will to 'be good' for the photographer? Are her fixed and staring eyes those of a subject under hypnosis, unable to be released until she is allowed?

For me, this photograph tellingly catches the ambivalence at the heart of the mother/daughter relationship, one which at its best is supportive and enriching, but which at its worst causes irreparable damage. Angelica Garnett, writing in her memoir, *Deceived by Kindness*, about the imminent death of her mother, Vanessa Bell, beautifully expressed her own paradoxical feelings: 'The thought that [my mother] might die was unbelievable, terrible and at the same time inadmissably exhilarating. Like the disappearance of some familiar monument, her absence would reveal a new perspective in which I might be able to find freedom.'

Most women I know feel they have to tread carefully in their dealings with their mothers. It seems that age makes this no easier, although I sense that as we grow older we try to make peace with our mothers, either by avoiding confrontation altogether or by finding the key, finally, to communicating at a deeper level. Some daughters, and they are the lucky few in my experience, are able to achieve a certain harmony in this relationship early on in their lives; some never manage to at all.

The complexities of my feelings about my own mother have hovered at the edges of my consciousness since I was fourteen or fifteen, from the time that I began to question what until then I had seen as her complete and undeniable authority; and I can't say that I've yet resolved these ambiguities. This is one reason why it excites me to read others' accounts. I can say *yes, that's me*, feel that shock of recognition, delight in the knowledge that others share similar experiences, that my conflicting feelings towards my mother – of irritation, frustration, love, admiration, anger and even hate – aren't dreadful, aren't unique. I'll live, and so will she.

The contributors to this collection approach the subject

from widely varying standpoints, and with an abundance of history to inform their stories. The themes explored are wide-ranging: a displaced child looks at the way in which this distance influenced her subsequent relationship with her mother; the holocaust is at the centre of four writers' lives, either by direct experience or at one generation's remove; the daughter of an alcoholic parent describes her childhood; English Edwardian middle-class values contrast strikingly with those of Texan railroad poverty on the one hand and peripatetic Australian opportunism on the other; a mother's divorce and the place her daughter expects to take in her affections as a result is touchingly examined; racism and differing cultural expectations in a mixed-race marriage underlie another's adolescence.

These daughters have found the subject both painful and difficult to write about, causing a mass of buried feelings to be brought to the surface. They have been worried about their mothers' reactions if their mothers are still living; equally, the ghosts of the past have hovered over those whose mothers are dead. But the candour of their accounts of this most complex and potentially mine-strewn alliance is refreshing. Laced through with wisdom painfully acquired, these tales of the mother-daughter rollercoaster throw new light on one of the central relationships in every woman's life.

The Independent

CAROLINE CARTER 1931–1990

Zoë Heller

One night when I was ten years old, a woman turned up at our house announcing that she was in love with my mother. She worked at the Camden Town offices where my mother was running a 'Save London Transport' campaign and she had been nursing her secret passion for several weeks. Now, she had decided to move in with us. While my mother and stepfather held a whispered conference in the kitchen (Mother: 'She's clearly disturbed.' Stepfather: 'I don't care. Just send her away.'), my sister and I wandered casually in and out of the living room, to inspect our visitor. She sat, lank-haired and morose, on the sofa, sipping a cup of tea. Her voice, when she spoke, was a curious sort of urgent drawl. We gazed at her, and then at each other, with a mixture of awe and slowly dawning glee. A genuine insane person in *our* house!

Eventually, my stepfather emerged from the kitchen and went off upstairs, leaving my mother to disappoint her admirer in private. To our disgust, we children were told to go away too and I, being the youngest, was sent to bed. Exiled to my bedroom, I fretted and fumed and strained for sounds of madness below. I am struck, now, by my indifference to the romantic aspect of this episode: this was my first exposure to the idea of Sapphic love and yet it hardly registered. Back then, I think, it seemed a matter of banal inevitability that people – even *ladies* – should be fascinated and enthralled by my mother. I saw her as a super-woman, swooping through life, and slaying all-comers with her charisma.

In the first place, she was beautiful. Not pretty, in the unobtrusive, domestic way that some other people's mothers were – but importantly beautiful, with long limbs and broad shoulders and pale, clever eyes. Photographs taken of her in her early thirties, with four children under the age of ten, have the improbable look of those on-location fashion shoots where the stylist rounds up a bunch of local snaggle-toothed kiddies and gets the gorgeous model to pose in their midst. Even without her beauty, though, my mother would have made people sit up and look. She had an intense, intimidating presence and she possessed that armoury of gesture and expression with which bossy Englishwomen have been wordlessly commanding respect for hundreds of years. One very early memory is of crossing the road with her at Oxford Circus and observing how she marched out from the crowded pavement, making the cars halt. She always walked with a fast, serious stride and would not tolerate a mimsier pace. 'Am I a leper?' she would demand, when her children lagged.

Reared on her example, I grew up thinking of beauty as something inextricably linked to the formidable – the first time I met a *silly* beautiful woman, I was startled. My mother was strong and very fit and given to nonchalant displays of athleticism. At the seaside, it was a point of honour with her to swim out further than anyone else. Warnings of sharks and currents served only to encourage her. Many times I sat on beaches, watching, in an agony of fearfulness, as she ploughed off into the twinkly horizon. (And always, when she came racing back out of the surf, she would throw herself glamorously down on to the sand exclaiming maddeningly, 'You should have come!'). According to family legend, she had fought a bull on her honeymoon after my father had refused a toreador's challenge to enter the ring himself. She had mocked my father's cowardice and he had unwisely suggested that he'd like to see *her* try it. But she often rebuked me when I was a child, for showing off. '*Ca suffit*,' she would say witheringly, the moment I began to caper. It only occurred to me much later that my exhibitionist inclinations might, after all, have been inherited from her.

More than any of her physical grandeur, however, it was my mother's hard, rather spiky intelligence that seemed to be the true source of her potency. She was a fearsomely clever woman and she enjoyed her fearsomeness: her intellectual tenet was 'rigour'. She valued tough, ironic argument and kept zealous watch for woolly or sentimental thinking. Most of life, in fact, could be divided into that which she deemed 'serious' and that which she dismissed as 'soppy'. My father used to claim that she had once told him he wasn't worth arguing with because he 'didn't have an educated mind'. My mother denied this, but we laughed anyway, acknowledging that the anecdote, even if false, told a truth about her. She was just as summary and exacting in her assessments of her children. Rather like Samuel Johnson's mother, who had 'too much good sense to be vain of her son', she never allowed maternal pride to befuddle her judgement. Nothing was more crushing, as a child, than to have your breathless account of an Amazing Fact met by my mother's coolly raised eyebrow. When I announced that I wanted to study English (an irremediably 'soppy' subject) at university, her scorn was intense. 'Oh darling!' she said impatiently, 'What do you want to be – a nice *literary editor*?'

She herself had studied PPE at Oxford in the early fifties. She had been held as one of the bright sparks – a dashing, sharp-minded and 'capable' woman, known, because of her communist leanings and her good looks, as the 'Body Politic'. It was felt that she would end up doing something important and worthy – running the BBC perhaps, or standing for parliament. But like many women of her generation, her ambitions got tangled up in the undergrowth of children and too many interesting little stopgap jobs. In mid-life, she was plagued by a sense of having squandered her education and talents – of having been allowed by her liberal Hampstead upbringing to neglect the acquisition of 'proper skills'.

From time to time, these feelings would overpower her and she would succumb to long, inky-black bouts of despair. (The other day, I found a large card that I must have bought for her when I was eight or nine. It had a Dick Bruna illustration on one side and on the other, in loopy, felt-tip script, I had written, *Dear mum, please dont be depresed*.) She worried that she had passed on her depressive tendency to me and whenever I got gloomy as a little girl, she would panic and feed me giant, brown, iron pills. That impulse – to stamp out in her children what she feared and disliked in herself – was not so different, I see now, from that which made her scornful of 'namby pamby' English Literature degrees. 'Soppiness' was really only ever a catch-all term for what she saw as her own weaknesses. If she was intolerant of

4

mechanical incompetence, it was largely because she secretly feared her own cack-handedness. (Asked how to perform a particular task, she would reply with a superior smile, 'It's an intelligence test' – a phrase which makes me dizzy with irritation to this day.) If she seemed to hold the sciences, manufacturing industry and pretty much all varieties of entrepreneurial endeavour in exaggerated esteem, it had a lot to do with what she felt had been neglected or undervalued in her own artsy, *bien-pensant* education.

In her forties, she did actually set up and run her own business, selling information about EEC regulations to companies and producing an audio business magazine. It ended up as a modestly successful concern, but it was a stressful way of making a living. For the few years that the business was in operation, her mood – and consequently that of our household – veered erratically between giddy optimism and horror of impending financial ruin. The latter always seemed to me to be preferable to the former – on much the same principle that the moment of nemesis in a tragedy is easier to watch than the dance of unknowing hubris which precedes it. In her bullish states, my mother would corner members of the family to explain feverishly the Big Deal – the million dollar, jackpot deal – that was on the very *precipice* of being done. Or, more heart-sinkingly, she would start drawing up plans on the backs of envelopes for new business ideas: door-to-door sales of fire extinguishers, an international telephone phrase book for business people, a compact, house-cleaning kit called a 'Flatmate'. The shade of Willy Loman floated over these plans, but none of us was brave enough to try to qualify my mother's enthusiasm. However much we feared the despondency that was certain to succeed the excitement and hope, we feared her indignant wrath far more.

My mother was an intemperate woman, given to tantrums

so dazzlingly and defiantly unreasonable it was hard not to admire them. They always began with a trembling – a gentle, all-over, body rustle – which made her look as if she had been plugged into something. This, for us, was a sign as terrible and sure as tinkling crockery in a disaster movie. Once begun, the tremble built rapidly to a violent, blurry vibration. My mother's fists would clench and her jaw would become fixed in a terrible, teeth-baring rictus. 'I. Will. Not . . . Have it!' she'd hiss. The effect was almost a caricature of rage, as if she had learned getting angry from watching cartoons. What happened next was variable: perhaps she would throw chairs about the room; perhaps she would sweep up armfuls of our possessions and throw them out of the front door; perhaps (this was the option we prayed for) she would order us from the house. But always – usually towards the peak of the fury – she would whirl towards one of us, pointing a Squeers-like finger and booming the terrible phrase, '*You* are the chief offender.'

Our attempts to give ourselves the advantage by making longer range forecasts of her temper were mostly in vain. While we knew some things that would ensure Mother's displeasure – the cat puking up on the living room floor, the fruit (that she had forbidden us to eat) going rotten, an insufficiently enthusiastic response to her cooking, the house being 'squalid', all the bread having been eaten, a shop assistant asking her to put her name and address on the back of a cheque – there was no corresponding set of circumstances that would guarantee her good spirits. In the end, we gave up trying to impose scientific order on a force of nature and simply tried to remain watchful.

My mother was not, I want to make clear, a monster – although she was often monstrous. Her shows of affection were as energetic and intense as her mad frenzies and she certainly did her time labouring in the salt mines of

maternal duty: laying on birthday teas with stripy straws and
Snoopy napkins; listening to the first faltering recitation of
Dr Seuss books; cutting our hair at the kitchen table in grue-
some, Plantaganet bobs; singing for us, with great music hall
brio, a song about vegetables.

> *Don't be cruel to the vegeta-bule*
> *Always take its part.*
> *Don't be cruel to the vegeta-bule*
> *Remember that the lettuce has a he-e-art.*
> *Don't split peas, if you please*
> *Just because they're tasty on your tongue*
> *And remember when you're eating Brussels sprouts*
> *You're robbing the cabbage of its young!*
> *(Have a banana.)*

I cite these things here in the spurious interest of 'balance', but as a child I didn't really see my mother's
beneficent moods as 'making up for' her violent furies, or
as proving her lovable 'after all'. It didn't occur to me to
debit and credit her account in that way, any more than a
Hindu would presume to praise only the sunnier personality traits of a capricious Hindu goddess. My mother's good
and bad qualities were, strictly speaking, indivisible. Her
arbitrary decrees, her crazy explosions, were necessary com-
ponents of her talismanic strength: the love of a calmer,
sweeter-natured mother would not have seemed so valuable.

Of course, I often hated her – or, more accurately, longed
not to love her. In my early teens, it seemed to me that my
father, from whom she had separated when I was five, was
clearly the parent of choice. He was a screenwriter who
spent the larger part of the year living abroad. Rich, single,
accoutred with all the totems of bachelor cool, and for most

of the time fascinatingly absent, he was an irresistible foil to
my mother. I remember visiting his St John's Wood flat in
the late seventies and staring into his refrigerator – a double-
doored, American import the size of a wardrobe. Inside,
there was a pot of caviar, a doll-size carton of quail's eggs, a
joint of palest pink roast beef, a box of German marzipan
and two bottles of champagne. I surveyed these items like a
Home Counties girl in wartime Britain receiving her first
glimpse of American army rations. At home, my mother's
fridge was filled with saucers of left-over macaroni cheese,
bowls of dried fruit that were 'being left to soak', family
packs of Cheddar cheese, tureens of butterscotch-flavour
Instant Whip and always – always – an ominous vat of sour,
lumpy yoghurt which she made herself in a 1970s gadget
called a 'Yogomagic'.

If my father appealed to my unfettered adolescent greed,
he also promised to reconcile the contradictory schoolgirl
desire for status *and* unexceptionable averageness. He provided glamour – turning up unexpectedly at my school gates
in his Corvette Stingray, whisking me off to buy ostrich feath-
ers at Biba – but always in conventional forms that
schoolfriends could comprehend, that kept the dread threat
of being thought 'weird' safely at bay. My mother, by contrast, was *always* threatening to taint me with weirdness –
standing up in cinemas to shout 'Propaganda!' at trailer
documentaries about Namibia, hitting me in front of my
friends, serving cut-up pieces of fish finger for breakfast,
holding up queues at Sainsburys while she questioned items
on her grocery bill. By the time I reached puberty, I was no
longer convinced of her universal appeal. Those aspects of
her personality that had appeared so exciting and extraordinary when I was ten now seemed ghastly invitations to
social humiliation. She came once to Paddington Station to
see me off on a three-week school trip to Northumberland

and when all the other parents gathered at the ticket booth to wave goodbye, she elected to run alongside the departing train, all the way to the end of the platform. 'What is she *doing*?' my friends asked as we watched her gallop along, waving and grimacing outside the window. I waved back at her disconsolately, thinking how hopeless it was to try to explain. '*I* don't know,' I shrugged treacherously.

I am ashamed when I recall how often during my adolescence I affected detachment and dismissed my mother as 'loony'. Since she died, four years ago, I have thought often and with regret about this cowardice, not least because the dangers of betraying her by parody now seem compounded. When she was alive, there was always a complicated, nuanced reality against which to check crude formulations about her bad temper or her 'madness'. These days, when I tell a jokey anecdote about my mother, or offer her up as an amusing 'character', I am aware that this account is all my audience will ever know of her. I find myself wanting to stop – to go back and qualify and complicate the tale. I worry that in the long run, when she ceases to seem merely absent, and becomes a proper ghost, I will begin to think of her in the impoverished terms of anecdote myself.

She first became ill in 1983, with cancer of the colon. After a year in hospital, and fifteen operations, she was pronounced well again, but the cancer had, in fact, retired to her lymph glands where it lurked for another five years before appearing in her lungs. From the moment the first cancer was diagnosed, it was clear that my mother's life was likely to be drastically foreshortened. But there were seven years between the initial diagnosis and her death at the age of fifty-nine, during which it became easy to imagine that she would be around for ever. This was partly because she was always, rather surprisingly, a gracious, stoical patient – anxious not to alarm her children with the severity of her pain,

9

or to drift into the solipsism that she saw as the worst aspect of invalid status.

In 1990, when she finally began dying in earnest, I had just started a new job on a newspaper and I was too self-absorbed to notice that she was staying in bed longer and longer each day; that, increasingly, she was not well enough to get dressed. My job was going badly and often, after work, I would go over to her flat and lie next to her in bed, weeping about how I couldn't do it, how my pieces were being spiked, how I would probably be sacked. As always, her response to her children's unhappiness was irritable sympathy, giving way rapidly to naked exasperation. 'Oh darling!' she would say, after cooing soothingly for a bit. 'Don't be a *ninny* about it.'

She could not quite believe she was dying. Again and again, she would begin to recede into her illness, only to resurface and be confusingly herself once more. In the last week before she died, she staged a miraculous, miniature recovery – got out of bed, tottered fiercely around the living room, ate some scrambled eggs, and signed the overdue pages of her sickness benefit book. ('I'm not going to let the buggers keep it,' she said when someone remonstrated mildly.) Two days before she died, when the cancer had gone to her spine and up into her brain, I sat on her bed helping her go through her jewellery box and write down which items should go to whom. She had always been a passionate list-maker – one of those people who find uses for the pages of coloured, stick-on dots and rectangles that you buy at stationers. This was the last list she made and it was never finished. She was moving in and out of coherence now. Her beautiful, very upright script had become chaotic and drunken; she kept writing down the names of those to be endowed and then forgetting who they were, or why their names were on a piece of paper. But whenever I offered to come back later, or showed any sign of not taking the project seriously, she would startle me by gripping the pen and snapping at me with angry, unmistakable sanity.

Her morphine dose rose and rose and her periods of consciousness became rarer. The day came when the family trooped into her bedroom to say goodbye. She was asleep, looking shrunken and bird-like in a pair of pyjamas that were now far too big for her. When she woke and saw us standing like a group of Victorian physicians, at the end of her bed, she smiled very broadly. One of us – I think it was my stepfather – said something about there not being much time left. She reared up in bed. 'But how do you know?' she said. 'I don't *feel* as if I'm going to die now.' Later, we went in separately to say our individual goodbyes. As I sat gulping and sniffing by her bedside, she raised herself on the little bony triangles of her elbows and gazed at me. 'Now darling,' she said, 'you will stick at the job, won't you?'

It is a rite of passage that takes place somewhere in your late twenties – the first time you look in the mirror and discover that yes, you too are destined to become your mother. I haven't inherited her great, glowing beauty. But my face and my legs have begun to develop the same angles and pockets of flesh as hers. My wrinkles are an imitation of hers. Even my teeth are starting to acquire a mother-ish aspect. The growing physical likeness is less startling, however, than the emergence of maternal mannerisms and vocabulary. You would think that whatever you'd picked up from your parents in the way of intonation and gesture would show itself early on, while you were in closest and most regular contact with the prototypes. Why is it only now, aged twenty-eight, that I feel my eyebrows rising and my lip curling into Mother's swerved smile of scepticism? That I have taken to filling *my* fridge with saucers of left-overs? That her key words ('chief offender', 'gumption', 'preposterous', 'ninny') have begun to bubble up, unbidden, into my mouth?

11

Perhaps, like the lifetime's supply of eggs stacked up in a female foetus's ovaries, a store of Mother-derived manners has always been lurking in me – a queue of behavioural tendencies on a slow, biological time-release. Perhaps next year, there'll be a whirr and a beep somewhere in my left cortex and, at the age of twenty-nine, I'll find myself wanting to swim far out to sea and berating shop assistants for asking me to write my address on the back of cheques. Becoming my mother is an odd process. Sometimes I look in the mirror, tracing the faint lines that wind away from the corners of my eyes, like tributary rivers on a map. I am, I realise, the best memento I have of her.

I LOVE MY MOTHER, BUT

Mira Hamermesh

The drizzly rain gave a wet shine to a dull October morning. The still life of a table set for breakfast which I later tried to capture in a painting could never have shown that the bread, mixed with sawdust, was bought on the black market and flaked when cut. Nor that the milk was diluted with water. Nor that my mother, standing at the stove, was cooking the last cupful of pre-war porridge oats left in the larder.

This ordinary domestic scene in our dining room took place at an extraordinary time, just after the outbreak of the 1939 war. The September blitzkrieg against Poland, and the subsequent invasion by two armies, the German and the Soviet, who between them divided Poland, had turned our lives upside down. Money had lost its value and Father was no longer a provider. It was dangerous for adults to go outdoors; it was safer for children. Jews, by degrees, were being deprived of civic rights. It was the end of October and we were still in our large flat, still eating off our fine china and using silver cutlery embossed with the family monogram. Essential foodstuffs were in short supply. A black market flourished and schools were shut.

This family breakfast was like so many before, except that none of us knew at the time that it was going to be our last meal together. Mother poured an unfamiliar substance into our cups, a new German-made brew, an ersatz coffee substitute. This novelty came with the invasion. It was bitter in taste and unfamiliar in appearance.

'We don't even know what goes into it; it could be harmful for the kidneys,' Mother said, carefully inspecting the bottle. Putting it down, she added in an agitated tone of voice, 'A perfect way to poison a whole people!'

'Mother!' I scolded her, shocked at the insinuation.

Father tried to soften the impact of her remark, but I knew better. Like a Cassandra, my mother was inclined to utter warnings about impending disasters.

'Mark my words, something terrible is going to happen! I feel it in my heart!'

She was again in the grip of fear, its origin lost in the obscurity of her past. The colour drained from her cheeks, her lips trembled and her eyes showed terror as she entered the territory inside her mind. The vision was planted with minefields, every minute could be a moment of some dreadful loss! Every street a potential road to catastrophe! Anything could happen after one put down the telephone . . .

I grew up riveted to my mother's fear of tomorrow, of next week, next month, next year. There were rivers which could burst their banks, mountains that could slide. Bombs might fall from the sky, leaving devastation in their wake. Mother's condition, her propensity for prophecy, was accepted by the family as a residue of her rabbinical ancestry. Luckily for her, Poland, a provincial country, was still remote from the shockwaves of Freudian psychology and the term paranoia or persecution mania. I used the war as an excuse to cut loose from the sweep of Mother's dark visions. I tore at the bonds of parental love, snapping attachments with teenage brutality. I drained off affection and made place for irritation and hate. Mother's thin lips laced my heart with frigidity, her kisses chilled me.

Now I just wanted to get away from home for a short time. I intended to come back to my pet dog Puppi, my books and diaries. It was never meant to be a final separation.

'Get away from what?' I was often asked when talking about leaving home. Mostly it was from the storms generated by Mother's sense of doom. But other explanations served the purpose better.

When I said I wanted to go to the 'other side', it was a schoolgirl's idea of adventure and liberation, blending an imaginary territory concocted from books and films with a concrete geography. On the map of the new political reality, on which sovereign Poland was obliterated, the 'other side' was the newly established German–Soviet border, which made neutral Romania accessible. But it could equally have meant the other side of the moon. I was in a hurry and wild to get away.

Mother was bewildered by the change in my personality. Overnight I had become restless and determined to leave home. From a bookish, home-loving thirteen-year-old girl, I was transformed into a character from an adventure story. I organised gangs of school friends to roam the streets, keen to challenge the anti-Jewish regulations announced daily. When a ban on travelling by tram was announced, we would

15

make a point of riding on trams, aimlessly, from morning until curfew. With cinemas declared out of bounds to Jews, we would start in the early afternoon, sitting through all performances, getting a bellyful of German films which mainly consisted of Nazi propaganda. I organised a break-in into the office of our school in order to secure the seals with which to fake 'gymnasium' certificates. I anticipated that documents offering a choice of false domiciles, in cities other than our native Lodz, might come in useful. As indeed it did in my case when I planned my departure to the 'other side'. I never knew that such impulses are termed by historians as 'Resistance'.

My family and neighbours had another view of my activities. 'Plain crazy', 'Out of control', 'The result of an over-active imagination'. How else were they to explain my idea of joining my older sister, who six months earlier had been sent to Palestine to agricultural school?

Mother wrung her hands and shouted at me. 'Day-dreaming again! Going to Palestine in the middle of the war? It's crazy! We must all stay together! If we die, we die together . . .'

That's exactly what I did not want to do. Not yet.

She burst into tears, angry with Father for not opposing my scheme. She complained bitterly about disobedient children. Father, the incurable optimist, tried to reassure her. 'Let her find out for herself that leaving home is no picnic! She'll soon come running back home. Just wait and see.'

For safety, he ordered my older brother to be my chaperone until our speedy return. Mother stared tearfully at the two of us. We were both fully dressed and ready with our backpacks for departure.

'You can still change your mind,' she pleaded. I was in such a hurry to get away that I did not finish the porridge or

16

the ersatz brew. At the door, Mother's embrace held me rigid against her, the grip tearing to shreds my resolve to leave. I knew if I let her hold me one minute more, I would never be able to tear myself away from her. Never! Her body was like a magnet, an invisible coil binding our flesh together. It was a moment of physical pain, lament and admonition addressed to heaven, her words impossible to forget.

'I will never see you again!'

I slid out from Mother's embrace, avoided looking at her face. Once on the other side of the door, I ran fast down the stairs, chased by her heartbreaking sobs.

'I will never see you again!'

Father accompanied us to the railway station. It was besieged by a huge crowd trying to get on the train. We were pushing hard to get through, my brother leading the way, Father behind us. It was like cutting through a solid human mass, held together by the sheer immensity of pressure.

'Remember, whatever happens, never, never separate! Always stay together!' Father's last-minute admonitions were drowned in the roar of the surging crowd. My brother, a tall lad, held our luggage above his head with one hand and with the other he pushed me towards the carriage. The distance between us and Father grew bigger as we fought to get on the train. Father's desperate efforts to get closer were hindered by the crowd storming the train. Somehow we managed to board and once in, squeezed ourselves towards a window. We waved to Father and watched him struggle, like a swimmer, steering himself against the human tide. He waved to us, holding up a small package wrapped in soft tissue. At the top of his voice he shouted his last message.

'Mother wanted you to have it!'

Much later we learned that it contained a few of Mother's

jewellery pieces which in the chaos he had forgotten to give us.

A sharp whistle made the train shudder and move. My brother, his arm outstretched, leant out of the window as far as it was possible without falling out. Father was making some progress in fighting his way to the train. Finally he managed to position himself level with the window. The train began to gather speed. Father ran after it as fast as he could, once more almost parallel to the window, but again was pushed away by people, who like him were running along the platform, also keen for a last contact with their dear ones. His manoeuvre to pass Mother's gift to us failed. Groping for the last link with his children, his attempt to reach my brother's hand was denied for ever. Seen from the moving train, my father's waving arms seemed already cut off from us and from the body of mankind.

I never saw Mother again. She died of hunger in the Lodz ghetto in May 1943. She was lucky not to have been carted off to the Auschwitz gas chambers, a fate which befell my father in the last week of the war.

The scene at the door has become fixed on my peripheral vision forever, rendering all doors, all separations, a descent to Mother's suffering.

Mother bore three children; her first-born a male, and two girls, of whom I am the youngest. She had the reputation of being clever and her advice was often sought out by others. A handsome woman, her only concession to glamour was a touch of Coty face powder applied with a giant puff, and two shades of lipstick. I loved her Crêpe de Chine perfume, which I would secretly dab on myself. In spite of her heavy build and swollen legs, she insisted on wearing fashionable court shoes with high heels in an attempt to enhance her majestic bearing. By Polish pre-war standards our family was ranked as well-to-do, but memories of childhood poverty and the resulting loss of face left Mother with a permanent feeling of insecurity.

Law abiding, paying taxes and, when necessary, bribes, Mother had no hidden vices. A non-smoker, non-drinker, her only weakness was an excessive devotion to her family and God. A religiously ingrained sense of righteousness informed her moral conduct. As a child, watching her at prayer in synagogue, I was sure Mother was on intimate terms with God and that her prayers were given special attention. The prayer book and the Bible were her only reading matter.

I grew up without any ancestral photos, letters, or documents which would have given me an idea of what my mother's parents or grandparents looked like. In the shifting fortunes of the Great War (1914–18), the house of Mother's illustrious grandfather, the Rebbe of Zgierz, was destroyed in bombardments, pillage and fire.

What my mother looked like before she married Father, I don't know. There is no one left to ask so I have to reconstruct a picture of her life before she became my mother. To fill the gaps, I snap up fragments of information, some remembered, some told many years after her death, and put them together like a jigsaw according to whim.

Mother often invoked her illustrious lineage. She took great pride in being the granddaughter of the Zgierz Rabbi. I am ashamed of my failure to have learnt more about my mother's background when I was still at home. What stories I missed!

What kind of person was this woman, known to me only as the provider of food and maternal care laced with an unpalatable taste of fear? What thoughts filled her head when she gazed at the wondrous moon sliding through the velvet sky? What dreams, what aspirations, filled her heart and mind before she became a wife and mother? Who were her Bible heroes, she who kissed the Bible and prayer books when they chanced to fall to the ground? What secrets did she hide, which so shattered the peace of her mind? What soul storms thundered through her, erupting into sonorous, heavy sighs? Oh, those sighs which used to fall upon me like a whip! And the tears, the aches and pains she tried to hide from her children. Were they echoes of an unhappiness belonging to another mental zone of her existence?

The unknown cannot be fully depicted, but there were rare moments when I saw glimpses of a happier person hidden inside my mother's body. Dancing at a Jewish wedding, looking radiant and joyful. Or the occasional afternoon visits by Bella, Mother's best friend. The memory of Bella shines in my mind with the glow of her gold-covered front teeth and her laughter cascading like rolling beads. How I would try to break up their intimate afternoons, filled with whispered shared secrets and peals of laughter as they sat sipping tea behind closed doors! These were glimpses of a different character to the one we were familiar with, the 'Mater Familia', a woman consumed by anxiety about the future of her children.

I often wonder who she would have become had her family history not been blighted by a fatal love story. It all began long before my mother was born, during the turbulent times after the 1863 Polish uprising against Tsarist Russia. The way the story came to me illustrates how the brew of life is fermented by the yeast of imagination. It weaves a tale of a Chassidic world in which holiness is enmeshed with curses, generosity with a meanness of spirit.

I am journeying into the territory of my mother's ancestral past, linking me to a world now totally vanished. Half reality and half legend, it invokes a time of Wonder Rabbis, of small towns built of wooden houses planted across the Polish rustic landscape. The family legend concerns mother's illustrious grandfather, the Zgierz Rabbi. Famed for his learning, his reputation as a wise and saintly man spread far beyond the boundaries of his town. Followers would travel from far and wide for the privilege of an audience with him.

His only son, Motke, was a bright and promising Talmudic student, a suitable candidate to continue the rabbinical dynasty. Fate intervened in the person of the local milkman, a humble widower, with a beautiful daughter named Golda. From early childhood, she used to accompany her father on his milkrounds. Sitting next to him, she was admired by neighbours for her beauty and charm. She often helped him, measuring and pouring the milk into the vessels provided by the customers.

It so happened that the task of collecting the milk often fell to the rabbi's son. Over the years, the two children became friends. The milkman cherished a secret hope that Motke would become attached to his daughter. To this end he used to offer Motke special treats, cheese cookies, a speciality for which he was famed. At the age of thirteen her father let Golda handle the reins of the carthorse as a sign of her maturity. Golda, who had already blossomed into a ravishing beauty, made Motke blush each time he saw her. The milkman's expectations were fulfilled. The teenagers were consumed by a romantic fever. At sixteen, the lovesick Motke was manoeuvred by the milkman into making a pledge, under oath, that he would marry Golda, come what may.

What followed was pandemonium. The household of the Zgierz Rabbi resounded with lamentations. After much fasting and praying, an ultimatum was given to Motke.

Renounce the promise given to Golda or you will be declared dead to the family! Banished! Cursed!

Torn between his love and respect for his father and his love for Golda, Motke couldn't decide. Unable to make a choice, the decision was made for him. The rabbi put a curse on his first-born son whom he mourned ritually as if dead. Motke was chased out of his father's house and chased from the town.

Disgraced and disowned, his spirit broke. The milkman nursed him back to health and Motke married Golda at the age of seventeen. He never recovered from the severance from his family and the loss of the splendour of his father's rabbinical court. He scraped a living with difficulty, as a low status teacher. Golda gave birth to seven children, five daughters, of whom my mother was one, and two sons. The family lived in grinding poverty, made worse by the shadow of the curse.

Motke died young, broken in body and spirit. By the age of thirty, Golda was left a widow. The responsibility for the upkeep of the family fell on her and the children. There was no schooling for the girls, only for the boys. The girls helped their mother to make ends meet. Worse than poverty and hunger was the shame of 'coming down in the world'. Mother and daughters were desperate to maintain the last shreds of dignity.

Towards the end of his life, Mother's grandfather relented and acknowledged his ill-fated daughter-in-law and his estranged grandchildren. By this time he was already an old, ailing man. Mother must have been about fifteen years old when she first crossed the threshold of the Zgierz Rabbi's house. Her head had been filled with stories told by her father about the splendour of Sabbath and Holy Day celebrations. The dining room, which could seat more than fifty people, was filled to overflowing with faithful Chassidic followers. The rabbi's upright chair, like a throne, stood at the head of the long table, covered with a white tablecloth. For the faithful, the table became transformed into a lane leading to a heaven of their own making.

For my mother, access to this privileged household came too late. Soon afterwards, the illustrious Zgierz Rabbi died. Golda and her children came into their inheritance, only to witness the decline of a once-venerated family. The rabbinical dynasty had come to an end.

That family saga goes a long way to explain why my mother, through the rest of her life, suffered a sense of injured pride and the fear of 'coming down in the world'. I suspect that memories of exile from the splendour of the Zgierz Rabbi's court and the disgrace of this had created a torture chamber inside her heart.

Folklore mixed with popular romanticism still filters through the lives of my mother's children and grandchildren. Even our names carry an echo of past lives. The name Motke, a diminutive of Mordechai, was given to my brother, my mother's first-born son. Genia, the Polish version of Golda, was given to my older sister. My own name, like everything else about my character, links me to my father's family. The biblical root of my name, Miriam, was given to me to honour another ancestral matriarch, my paternal grandmother.

From behind the shadow of the past, our ancestors' ravings, loves and curses step out to meet a shared future. A less lethal version of the Zgierz Rabbi's curse popped out of Mother's mouth when my sister, aged eleven, went on strike, refusing to eat what was put in front of her. She also stopped talking to Mother. Outraged by her rebellious obstinacy, true to ancestral form, Mother uttered something which resembled a curse. 'When you become a mother, may your own daughter cause you as much aggravation!'

My sister's obduracy proved temporary, for within a couple of years she became a model of filial devotion. But the potency of Mother's utterance proved fatal. From the day of her birth, my niece was difficult to raise and my sister viewed everything about the child's personality as a provocation. Later on in life, the rift continued. As a teenager, she careered out of control, seduced by a teacher. Her turning her back on higher education was a severe blow to my sister's hopes. From then on, my niece's numerous marriages and divorces added sparks to the friction. An unhealing wound festered in the hearts of both mother and daughter.

It was in my older sister that my mother has fully implanted herself genetically. Whenever our paths cross, I recognise in her rounded grey eyes and small mouth Mother's expression of permanent anxiety and a sense of life fatigue. Mother's unnamed grief has become hers, so have Mother's aches and pains which have imperceptibly shaped her body into the heavy maternal mould. My sister's swollen feet and shoe-induced agony, including the accompanying moans, replicate Mother's when she changed shoes after walking.

Perhaps it's not by chance that she most resembles Mother in body and soul. Like Mother, she suffers from the dread of 'losing face'. Her whole life has been devoted to an illusory idea of holding the 'family' together and restoring its lost social lustre. It's a heritage of unnamed despair and suffering, passed on wordlessly from mother to daughter.

Have I really managed to escape it?

When I was younger, I did not understand the kind of hold mothers have on women's lives. Consciously or unconsciously our mothers' unfulfilled dreams, frustrations and bitternesses repeat on us like chronic psychic indigestion. Each woman has the role of an archaeologist imposed on her, digging into the debris of a buried past, retrieving the fossils embedded in the soil of our origins.

My own life stands like a bridge linking two distant shores separated by the turbulence of history, the vagaries of genetic and cultural mixing. I have established roots in England through marriage to an Englishman. The birth of my son made my body a link in the chain of history, a meeting point of two geographies and two cultures. My mother's lineage runs through the Polish soil and a tortured history. It charts Poland's decline from a European power to a country parcelled out between three enemies: imperial Russia, Austria and Germany. My son's English heritage encompasses the history of a small island which evolved from a Roman occupied province into a United Kingdom with an imperial past. The legacy of the Second World War, though shared by Poland and England, has left a different impact on its peoples. The deep divide is symbolised by Auschwitz and other concentration and death camps located on Polish soil and by the destruction of European Jewish communities.

Life in England, the passing years and events, sifted over the memory of my leave-taking from Mother. In the act of forgetting, part of me was buried in her tomb, which I had never seen. The first awakening in my consciousness of Mother's presence came to me via a dream, shortly before my own confinement. In it, my mother lay in a transparent grave. A shrub was growing from her breasts, she was feeding life again. I plucked a shoot from the shrub. While holding it, my hand turned into a flowering branch.

How was I to know, as I lay stretched out on the delivery trolley in a London maternity ward, that in between labour contractions, while pushing out a new life, the movement would stir the spirit of my dead mother? That the dark content of death gave off sparks which illuminated the emergence of new life? We know so little about the mysterious bond between the living and the dead, between soul and soul.

With each spasm I cried out for my mother with a renewed longing, the pain of labour uniting us again. Summoned by my cries, my mother materialised at my bedside. As they cut my son's umbilical cord, I felt my mother's eyes fixed upon us with an unblinking gaze. An avenger, my mother's avenger was born! The first time I held the baby in my arms, I felt the weight of the sorrow of war press down on both of us. At that instant I understood how women's wombs become the rendezvous point of birth and death.

Years later, at the age of five, my son asked a childish question which steered me deeper into the impenetrable mystery of my own survival. 'Mum, where do the dead go?'

I had to acknowledge to myself that often they don't 'go' anywhere. They just patiently wait to be acknowledged. Perhaps every moment of time once lived by the dead remains hanging in the air around us. The longevity of the dead may have to be measured in different units of time.

I am often classed as a survivor, in spite of the fact that I was far away from the places of destruction. But my name was on the list, and had I stayed on I too would have been deported to Auschwitz. The kind of difficulties survivors of catastrophes face lie less in their dealings with the living than in their uneasy relationship with the dead. The balancing act of attempting to satisfy the needs of the living with the demands of the dead makes emotional life precarious. In addition, there is always the nagging question, which seeps like poison into one's existence. 'Why me? Why not any of my school friends, as bright if not brighter than myself?' Common opinion holds a view that the best, the noblest perish, and the survivors belong to a ruthless and ignoble breed. Maybe yes, maybe not. The absence of logic when trying to penetrate the impenetrable equation makes the survivor a hero at the heart of a mystery. The survivor lives on the edge of omnipotence or fatalism. In the intervention of the Fatum, the dead hitch a ride. Loving the dead sends one's affection into an endless exile.

Nearly forty years later, in *Loving the Dead,* a film I made for the BBC, I finally tackled the theme of how the dead affect the living. The film explores how the Jews are remembered in present-day Poland. It begins with the search for my mother's grave in the ghetto section of the Jewish cemetery in Lodz. The film was shot in winter. The shrubs which fed off my mother's body were turned by the frost into icy crystals. The image of Death with a Scythe was replicated by the Polish cemetery keeper whose scythe cleared the overgrown grounds. The mood of the film was embossed with the seal of my mother's unfulfilled dreams.

A posterity of sorts is secured for our fathers, alive or dead, by bureaucracy. It took me a while to realise the gaping omission regarding our mothers. Once it sunk into my awareness, I decided to correct it. Whenever I had to deal with the formalities of filling in forms, be they job or visa applications, in offices or at consulates, when flying or landing, confronted with the question about the name of my father, I would add, unsolicited, my mother's name, even if the act of protest consisted only of scribbling her name in the corner of the questionnaire. This urge stemmed from my rage that officialdom was robbing my mother of a chance of a bureaucracy-generated posterity.

When I told a friend about this, he expressed his admiration for the depth of my feelings. 'How you must have loved her!' He was deeply shocked when I admitted having ambivalent feelings towards Mother. Yes, I loved my mother, but . . . I remember, as a child, often being teased by neighbours with the question, 'Who do you love more, Mummy or Daddy?' Like most children put in this awkward situation, I did not tell the truth. 'I love them both equally,' I protested, whereas in truth I regarded myself to be more of Father's than Mother's daughter. A classic case of a 'daddy's girl'.

There were so many 'buts' in my mother–daughter relationship. Mother was a disciplinarian and Father was indulgent. She sighed a lot, her bosom heaving, oozing discontent and unhappiness. Father whistled, smiled often and looked a happy man. With him the time passed quickly, full of activities and chatter. With Mother time lingered, her statuesque body moved slowly, her silences as much a reproach as her scolding words. Her pride and aloofness made me envy friends whose mothers were easy-going with their children, demonstrative in their affection.

Only at night did I love my mother absolutely. Sharing her bed, the maternal body which engulfed me in its warmth and scent filled me with a sense of security and bliss. Even in the intimacy of sharing a bed her flesh signalled an aura of majesty which explained in part her distance from childish things. She was a good mother, devoted to her children and home. We were well fed and dressed, and were kept neat. There was no nonsense about toys, stories or hugging us. Only during an illness did I feel her hot, anxious love, and was sorry when I quickly recovered.

I sometimes look at myself in the mirror, searching for traces of Mother's features in my face or in the contours of my body. The youngest of her three children, I alone resemble Father in looks and temperament. I once tried to paint a posthumous portrait of Mother. It proved difficult for reasons that had little to do with the composition. I intended it to become an icon of martyred motherhood, but it refused to hold together. Against my will and control, it kept splintering into separate details.

Like, for instance, Mother's made-to-measure satin corset, reinforced with whalebones. This exquisite undergarment, in shocking pink, adorned with lace and miniature rosebuds, encased her corpulent body like armour. As a child I would steal into her bedroom and secretly admire the impressive construction which would stand on the floor by itself, as if it had a life of its own. It represented a forbidden trophy of womanhood, a regal shield of a warrior queen both desirable and frightening. Watching myself in the mirror, I would step inside it, pull the laces as tightly as I could, feeling lost in its vastness. I wondered how my mother's generous, fleshy breasts managed to nestle, like birds, inside the upholstered cups.

On a recent visit to the Auschwitz Museum, I found similar corsets on display amongst other artefacts of historical importance which include heaps of twisted frames of glasses and children's artificial limbs. The few tattered, corroded corsets, showing rust where once there were metal reinforcements, grasped my attention with a new tenacity.

There, I understood why the intended icon to martyred motherhood refused to materialise on my canvas. The image, not only of mother's corset in Auschwitz, but also of her jewellery, fur coats, hats, all requisitioned by the *Wehrmacht*, became an obstacle which stood between my painterly vision and the brush. The pink, satin corset of a fat, middle-aged Jewish mother had no place in the iconography of serious European art. Only in surrealism could this find an expression. But I was a realist. The space on canvas no longer invited my inspiration. My passion for painting was dislodged. The transition to film-making released my power of self-expression again. Only on the screen can I envisage a version of a *Pietà* in which a woman like my mother, imprisoned in a corset, laments the death of her hopes and dreams.

Much as I strain, I fail to find in the mirror any visible resemblance to Mother. Nevertheless, some aspects of her life have deeply lodged inside the cells of my body and psyche. She is the matrix which produced my psychosomatic manifestations. The connection between the psyche and body being so strong, it's not only by chance that I have developed a serious back problem. Was my mother at the root of the unconscious reason why I have incorporated surgical corsets into my own existence?

After twenty years of chronic back pain, before I had a neuro-surgical operation, I too accumulated in my wardrobe a collection of made-to-measure corsets. The difference was in the choice of colour. Mine were also made of shiny satin, not pink, but black. Very sexy, my lover thought, neither of us realising the tragic association my condition represented.

I live with the idea of two mothers. The wartime mother and the before-the-war mother, surviving inside the shell of her corset. A woman who visited the hairdresser regularly, her mousy-coloured hair waved with hot tongs. My nostrils will flare when I stand near women smelling of scents which remind me of Mother's Coty powder and French perfumes. How I loved shopping with her for the fine fabrics which she would select and take to her 'little dressmaker'! There, looking through the latest English fashion journals, I encountered a world populated by thin tall men and women holding on to equally slim, long-legged racing dogs.

Mother travelled regularly to Marienbad to 'take the waters'. Once she left behind on the train her favourite black velour cardinal-shaped hat. What a calamity! This made a deep impression on me. The story led me to weave numerous adventures about Mother's hat travelling all on its own, crossing borders, seeking its owner. The distressed hat, like a huge black bird, landed aggressively on women's heads, terrifying them! Poor Mother! Poor hat! My fantasies were cut short weeks later when the hat was sent back from Romania to Poland, where it was finally reunited with Mother. Inside my imagination, that black hat still travels in circles. This may explain my own passion for hats, and my search for the perfect black hat, made of softest felt, with a large brim.

I owe the richness of my imaginative flair to my desperation to get Mother's attention. To this end I learned to use it in a variety of ways. Sent out to buy a box of matches, I would return with a tall story. A horse slipped on the cobbled street, a regular enough event, but in my version there was drama and surprise. The driver whipped the horse so hard that it died. Or it sprang to its feet like a mythical beast and kicked the cart driver to death. I would elaborate on things I saw, enlarging on them, making them exotic. Like, for instance, the time when a circus came to town and the procession passed our street. I ran home to tell of an escaped tiger hiding in our cellar. But I soon learned that Mother responded best to stories about orphans, beggars, miraculous reunions, lottery winnings, fortune-tellers predicting a prosperous future, and dream omens.

Once or twice she took me to her native town where she regularly visited the graves of her parents and grandparents. She would cry and unburden herself, talking to them in Yiddish, her native tongue. My brother and sister understood it, but I, the youngest, had already assimilated Polish. The linguistic barrier may be responsible for the absence of Mother's voice inside my head.

I could never imagine Mother as a child. Never! In my imagination she began life as a beautiful young maiden with two long blonde plaits reaching down to her hips. In her native town, young women were often terrorised by hooligans who liked nothing better than to snap their scissors and cut off the treasured tresses.

It feels very odd to be older than one's own mother. Our roles are now reversed. I, a mother in my own right, have become her sanctuary. She seeks from me an explanation for why she was condemned to die, of all things, a 'militarised death'. History has bestowed upon her a significance that her life never intended. Mother's unspent life has carried me along a path which my personality may never have intended for me either. It has generated in me hidden energies, unrelated to my artistic talents, but necessary if I am to confront the fall-out of the Final Solution. On Mother's behalf, I have undertaken an intellectually difficult quest to explain to myself and others why the chromosomes, hormones and genes of women like my mother were earmarked for destruction. By what military logic did the German war machinery, in the middle of a desperately difficult offensive on three fronts, make the capture and execution of such women a priority?

Mother has been dead since 1943, but in my consciousness she refuses to become a cadaver. I did not see her as a corpse, I did not follow her funeral. At the age of forty she just vanished from my life. In the absence of the customary rituals of the exit-from-life, she lingers on. So does her prophetic suspicion about man-made substances which can poison whole nations.

The mother whose image is stamped with wartime martyrdom is a phantom, changing shape. Sometimes, she resembles Demeter, stomping through the earth, lamenting and raving at the cruel fate which separated her from her children. At other times, too heavy to protect me as winged angel, she stays close to the ground. She nestles inside my shadow, measuring my steps and the direction I am taking in life.

I have never been able to come to grips with the mother locked inside a ghetto, dressed in rags, so tormented by hunger that her garments hang on her like a tent. The sensation of her hunger gnaws at my stomach, the acid of her pain seeping into my system.

Don't ever ask me if I love my mother!

Sally Soames

IN PARENTHESIS

Georgina Hammick

I, my dear, was born to-day –
So all my jolly comrades say:
They bring me music, wreaths, and mirth,
And ask to celebrate my birth . . .

I first came across Matthew Prior's *On My Birthday, July 21* in
the (Quiller–Couch) *Oxford Book of English Verse,* that is to say,
in the copy my mother gave me; and I remember thinking
'but that's her birthday!' – as though it couldn't possibly be
anyone else's. This is odd because, having a twin sister, my
birthday was always shared, never just mine, never just hers,
ours. My twin, Amanda, and I felt guilty as children about
using the singular possessive in matters that concerned, or
that could be perceived as concerning, both of us. This
Oxford anthology, however – India paper edition – was my

35

mother's present to me on our thirteenth birthday, 24 May 1952. I wrote my name in it without delay. Books were, apart from the drawing paper and pencils, chalks and crayons we always wanted and always got, the ideal presents to give us. Not just because we enjoyed sniffing the pages and even reading them, but because a book was an individual thing, chosen with one, not both, of us in mind. Whereas the other sorts of birthday and Christmas presents we received – kaleidoscopes, alarm clocks, badminton rackets, unpromising cardigans – were invariably in duplicate, as identical to look at as we were ourselves. I asked my mother about this not long ago, a loaded question no doubt, one that implied grave mistreatment over years. My mother said she hadn't dared give us different presents. (She put great emphasis on 'dared'.) She'd tried it once with dissimilar dolls, but one of us, not named, had preferred the other's doll to the one she'd been given, and then there was a punch up: hair pulled out, blood drawn, sororicide almost. My mother, our mother, shuddered at the memory. We were hell at the best of times, she assured me, and there weren't many of those. We called each other 'beast' and 'batty pig' all day long. Our favourite word was 'unfair'. We were farouche in the presence of strangers and grown-ups. We were 'enough to frighten the French'. We were tyrants who caused five governesses in succession to dash for the front gate after less than a week of our company.

My mother was born, as I've said, on 21 July. The year was 1912. I like the shape and, more especially, the sound of 1912: benign and serious and satisfying, it sounds to me – to half of me – *Nineteen twelve*. Two of my female heroes, Kathleen Ferrier and Elizabeth Taylor, the writer, whose novels and short stories my mother, also, admires, were born that year. But there's another face to 1912, a dark face, not benign at all: this was the year the *Titanic* went down. The inconceivable happened on the 15th April; so when Kathleen Ferrier – like my mother, a 'Lancashire Lass' – was born a week later on the morning of the 22nd, the front pages must still have been full of it: of black-framed photographs and lists; of haunting or heroic personal stories; of how-and-why questions. Not knowing Elizabeth Taylor's exact date of birth, I can't link it with the death of the *Titanic* in this dramatic, or ghoulish, way; but by the time my mother was delivered into the arms of her nurse, the *expensive* and, as it turned out, *delicate* ship had been on the ocean bed three months, her loss the subject of official enquiries but no longer headline news; the loss of her passengers of real concern only to the bereaved.

The Christian name my grandparents gave their eldest daughter and second child was Patricia, an aristocratic name that – if you add an 'n' – evokes classic sunshine, virile togas, gold sandals, cold marble floors. Not aristocratic by birth, my mother can appear grand. And in profile at least, her features – good forehead, straight nose, chiselled mouth, well-defined chin – may be said to be patrician. (Her eyes, which I've inherited, are small, but this isn't obvious sideways on.) My mother was the second of four, and the others – Peter, one year older, and Virginia and Caroline, five and ten years younger respectively – were given two names each. My mother didn't mind being singled out for singularity: in her view, a sole Christian name was original and distinguished, and when it came to our Christenings she did the same for us. By 'us' I mean Sarah, her first-born, Amanda and me. Twelve years later, when Henrietta turned up, my mother changed her mind (perhaps my father had something to do with this) and, in compensation for those missed opportunities, gave her youngest three names, one of them Patricia. (But then, as we saw it, all the rules were broken when

rietta was born.) That my mother has only one given
name is a fact, fixed in copperplate on her birth certificate,
but in a sense you could say she has, or has had, five. She was
Patsy when a baby, and at kindergarten; Pat in her teens as a
schoolgirl at the Mount School, York; Pattie to my father
and, eventually – taking their lead from their loved brother-
in-law – to her sisters also. As a widow in middle age, and
while old friends were writing letters to 'Dearest Pat', she was
encouraging new friends and acquaintances to call her
Patricia. Or Tricia. To those not fond of diminutives she's
been Patricia all along. So which is she, really? Which does
she most feel herself to be?

'Pattie,' my mother says without hesitation, 'because it's
what your father called me.' Then she says, 'Oh, and
Patricia. Yes. Not Pat though, it's jolly-hockey-sticks.
Certainly not Pat.'

I have a studio photograph of my mother and her brother,
taken when they were two and three. Somewhere the other
side of the Channel the British Expeditionary Force is having
a hard time, but you'd never guess this from the photographer's invented nursery, in which a pile of toy building bricks
hints at an unshakeable future, without a lead soldier or
stretcher bearer in sight. Peter and Patsy Marsh (their
mother's maiden name was Ridge, making the marriage a
fusion of incompatible geologies) are seated on cushions
and dressed in party clothes. My mother, her eyes to the
right, watching the birdie perhaps, looks wistful and shy, and
holds a doll in her lap. Her brother, eyes front, breezy smile,
a building brick in his left fist, appears confident. Examining
this photograph for the first time in years, I was struck most
by the clothes – little Patsy's white lawn frock and lace-
trimmed underskirts, little Peter's knickerbockers and
embroidered tunic, the spotless knee socks of both – and

what hell they must have been to launder. A picture of the red, shiny, 'Liverpool' brick outhouse at my grandmother's house in Freshfield came into my head. My memory of it goes back to the Second World War, but it can't have been very different in the First. It had steps up to it as I recall, and inside there were two Belfast sinks, a copper, an outsize mangle and any amount of scrubbing brushes and bars of green soap and packets of starch and galvanised buckets. Despite the steam, it was cold in there even in summer, and it had a sour, sulphurous smell, to do with washing soda and bluebag, but also, the coal house being next door, to do with coke and coal. Amanda and I would grace the wash-house from time to time to watch, and occasionally 'assist' (we liked working the mangle) Barbara and Margaret, the maids. In winter it was so icy your fingers fell off after five minutes, so we didn't stick at it for long. But then, unlike Barbara and Margaret, we didn't have to.

'I was an outgoing, busy – bossy if you like – child, very sure of what I thought,' my mother recalls. 'My brother, whom I adored, was not so sure, and used to sit on my head in the nursery. If I beat him at Ludo he'd sit on my head. Another thing he did was shut me in the top-floor cupboard.' She attributes her lifelong claustrophobia to these early experiences. The characters she describes, however, don't quite tally with the Peter and Patsy of the studio photograph; so I examine it again, and find that Peter's breeziness is much less certain than at first – his (too wide?) smile can be interpreted as a bully's nervous grin. Patsy's diffidence, looked at another way, seems archness merely, a coquettish pose adopted with the photographer in view.

'You say you adored Peter, but why?' I ask my mother. 'How do you adore someone who's always sitting on your head and shutting you in a cupboard?'

'He was so good-looking.' There's no irony in her reply; she means it. Appearances matter to my mother. How people, clothes, hair-dos, houses, dogs, look, is very important. More important, probably, than it is for most of us. For years now my mother has had one or two miniature Cavalier King Charles spaniels at her heels. It's inconceivable that she would own a mongrel.

But to get back to Peter: when he wasn't doing 'these nasty things', they had a lot of fun together. 'I wanted to be in his good graces,' she says. 'We were an item.' ('Item' sits strangely with 'good graces'. I forgot to ask, but imagine she picked it up from her grandchildren, or else from *Brookside* to which she's addicted.)

My mother has had women friends throughout her life, strong friendships that mean a lot to her, and whose loss – for she's outlived many of her closest – she feels keenly. Even so she's without question a 'man's woman', and what she has to say about Peter is in keeping with this. By 'man's woman', I mean someone not just attractive to, and attracted by, men, but for whom men are the be-all and end-all, and life without one is not life to any degree.

Given her attitude to men, and because her own marriage was happy, it's not surprising that the breakup of her three eldest daughters' marriages was a blow to my mother, as has been our 'failure' to remarry or to share our lives with a male partner (as, for the past twenty years, she has shared hers). She minds for us, who don't want her to, but also (you get the impression) for herself. Wishful thinking causes her to label any man we happen to mention a 'lover', and she'll do this even with men who, she has been told, are senile, say, or homosexual. 'How's the lover?' (or even 'How are the lovers?'), a favourite, light-hearted, conversation-opener of hers, can sound like something a lot heavier and more threatening. 'Naked at present, and tied to the bedposts', is probably the reply that would give most pleasure.

I wish that my mother could feel less negative and more relaxed about my two sisters' and my single state, but it seems that she can't; it's just too foreign to her. There's no knowing how many times one or other of us has been forced to explain that it really is possible to lead an 'all right' life without one of these 'glorious' male creatures in the home; that, say we would, ideally, like to be married, there simply aren't too many attractive/intelligent/amusing/kind spare men around when you get to our age who might want *us* (those that do exist are frequently into eighteen-year-olds); that the upside of loneliness is freedom, infinitely preferable to being stuck with the hideous furniture and three-hot-meals-a-day, bed-at-nine routine of (old) Mr Wrong; that we have our work; that we have our children; that we have our friends. At the end of these weary rehearsals she'll say 'Yes, yes, I do see,' but her tone is wistful, unconvinced. We could win Nobel prizes in all categories, climb Mount Kilimanjaro in record time, be the first to land on Mars, and she'd be proud of course, as she is of our actual achievements – but real success would be a wedding ring.

My mother, eighty-two this year (1994), is 'slowing up a lot now', she says. And it's true that, after a second hip replacement, operations for cataract and glaucoma, and with high blood pressure, fibrositis, plus an increasingly frail and painful backbone, she's noticeably less active than she was five years ago. She's stoical about this, brushing off enquiries and making light of pain. Despite the problems it's hard to think of her as old; she gives the appearance of being smaller than she used to be, but doesn't look her age, and never has done. Good luck must come into it, and a comfortable, privileged life, but also good management: since her twenties she's taken care of her frame in ways others would a prized motor car, 'keeping the show on the road', as she puts it, with spot checks and overhauls; with massage, chiropody and – increasingly complex – dentistry (with the result that her teeth are, almost all, her idiosyncratic own). As children we were banned from her bedroom during the massage and 'beauty treatment' sessions. (It was our father's bedroom too, but he was a soldier and away a lot so we thought of it as hers.) If we put our heads round the door we'd be rewarded by the astonishing sight of Eileen, the masseuse, slapping our mother's face and chin with good hard slaps, or pummelling some other, naked and fleshy, part of her. Later our mother would lie back on the pillows, her head in a turban, her face ghostly with face-pack, one hand outstretched while Eileen did her nails. I watched of course but found the whole thing bothering: the semi-secrecy of the rituals; my mother's eyes, two green-black bruises in the cracking mask; the punishment (it looked like punishment) of her body; the anointing of it afterwards with creams and lotions. For a full hour when Eileen was at work, my mother changed character. She became someone passive and submissive and somehow not quite real – a dummy or a doll perhaps.

I've never had massage or beauty treatment in my life, and so far haven't felt tempted to. It could be that the scene I've described has put me off; or it could be that as all 'body enhancement therapies' must entail removing your clothes I'd never have gone in for it anyway.

If, despite massage, my mother is slowing up, her brain-box appears not to be. Mellower than in the past, more resigned to things she does not care for but recognises she cannot alter or control, she still has strong opinions on some matters, and her long-term memory is extraordinary –

as I discovered when I went to 'interview' her for this piece.

On the car journey from my house to hers I had misgivings, not just about the prospect of asking her questions she might not like, or of hearing answers I might not like, but about the project itself. The difficulties which I hadn't properly considered when I accepted the invitation, and which must apply in some degree to every contributor to this collection, are legion, and here are a few of them: how do you begin to write about your mother (for God's sake)? How do you write about yourself in relation to your mother? How do you get the tone right, and the balance – or tell the 'truth' about anything? (My truth, for example, is unlikely to be my mother's truth, as it may not be my three sisters'.) Then there's the problem of selection: what to say that might be of interest to more than just the two of you; what aspects of her life and yours can or can't, should or shouldn't, be aired. (In print, remember; in a book that anyone – friend, foe, relation, stranger – can pick up and read.) Finally: how, if neither the snaky nor sentimental, confrontational nor confessional, approach seems exactly the right one, do you avoid whitewash or compromise – blandnesses that, apart from making dull reading, must in themselves imply betrayal of sorts?

Driving – due East, over Salisbury Plain – to my mother's house, the words pitfall, minefield, tightrope, nightmare, came into my head, together with bigger and better clichés such as 'can of worms', 'hornet's nest', 'Pandora's box' and 'painting oneself into a corner'. (Later, my daughter Kate came up with another: 'Aren't you playing with fire?' she asked me over the telephone. 'Thank God I don't have to write about *you*.')

I must stop this detour, and get my car through my mother's gateway and into her immaculate drive, taking care to drop speed to a crawl round the Pear Shape so there's no danger of even one stone of gravel landing on its grass (it might wreck the mower when Ken comes to mow). The edges and hedges in this weedless front garden have the razored precision you associate with municipal parks. My mother can be teased about this, and on occasion will mock herself for what she calls 'suburban' tidiness – although she makes it sound a virtue all the same. Her house, which I'm standing in front of, dates from 1712, is square and built of brick. It has stone facings, a white portico and a slate roof whose overhang, it always strikes me, is a bit on the big side, giving the impression of a handsome, but borrowed, hat. It's a pretty house, with a long walled garden (borders and fruit trees, old shrub roses, gravelled paths) at the back, and was my parents' dream when they moved here in 1959. My sisters and I thought the house too pretty, though. We'd imagined something less obvious, more mysterious, less kempt, more romantic.

> *Close and slow, summer is ending in Hampshire,*
> *Ebbing away down ramps of shaven lawn where close-*
> *clipped yew*
> *Insulates the lives of retired generals and admirals*
> *And the spyglasses hung in the hall and the prayer-*
> *books ready in the pew . . .*

These opening lines of Louis MacNeice's long poem *Autumn Journal* might have been written with my mother's surroundings in mind, which proves the accuracy of MacNeice's observation. The county's right, and the mani-cured garden; and my father was a retired general – about to start work for an American company – when they took the place over. He was a sidesman in the village church, St Peter-in-the-Wood (so presumably it was his job to get the prayer books ready in the pew); and, though a shy man, he read the lesson on Sundays. Close-clipped yew failed to insulate his life, however. In 1964 his 'summer' began to ebb away, and the following year he died here, of cancer, five days after his sixtieth birthday.

Often, on my way to or from London, I call in on my mother, and often, if I haven't warned her first, I can't get in. Because, at their age, my mother and her partner, The Colonel, are vulnerable; and because of past burglaries and attempted burglaries (during a successful one, of family portraits, thieves stole an 18th century husband from his wife), the place is now treble-locked. Today, though, my mother's expecting me, and the front door is on its latches. It's early March and freezing, and a relief to discover when she welcomes me that she's lit the drawing-room fire. Her house is cold in winter, at least I find it so, the hall exuding a damp chill that the cylinder-gas fire takes the edge off but cannot cure. My mother and The Colonel can get a 'good fug up' in the 'telly room', and hibernate there in the cold-est months; elsewhere, you feel, the atmosphere simply is not warm enough for octogenarians, both these prone to chest infections, one having arthritis in nearly every joint. Wouldn't they be better off in something smaller they could afford to heat? What's the point of all those empty bed-rooms, those extra bathrooms no one ever has a bath in but which someone – 'daily lady' in my mother's parlance – must be paid to clean? My sisters and I think these questions but don't ask them. It's not our business, strictly speaking, and we know the answers anyway. My mother doesn't want to move. She likes living in a big house. (Not *the* big house, however; in a village that boasts several large Queen Anne/Georgian houses, this one must rank as middle-sized.) And she likes living in this particular big or middle-sized house because she's used to it; its memories and associations make her feel 'safe'. Not hoping to die, she hopes to die in the house as my father did, in the bed they shared that he died in.

I've brought a tape recorder with me for this interview. It's twenty years old, so hardly state-of-the-art, but my mother is impressed. Unlike me, she's sanguine about our enterprise, seemingly looking forward to her part in it. When, after some testing – 'Am I too loud? I'm not sure if I've got the hang of this; am I doing this right?' – she gets going, she's like the runaway train of the song, no stopping her. (What I've asked her to do is this: talk about her background, parents, childhood, schooling, marriage, motherhood, etc. – any aspect of these, anything that comes into her head. I'll interrupt her from time to time, I've warned her, to ask specific questions. And though it's likely only a fraction of what's said will find its way into my piece, none of it will be wasted: this record of her life and thoughts will be of interest to her grandchildren.)

Not unnaturally, I hope my mother will say something about her mother, and eventually she does. I should say here that I wasn't fond of my grandmother Marsh and neither were my sisters; certainly she gave no indication that she was fond of us. My mother describes her as 'a loner, a one-off, withdrawn', who at the Mount School, York (the Ridges lived not far away, on the moors above Huddersfield) was 'keen on Latin and Greek, bookish, not gamesy at all'. Marriage to my grandfather, occupied all day with the family jute business in Bootle and with cricket every summer evening and weekend, meant – for there was nothing to do at home save order the meals and read – she was often bored and frustrated. 'A Madame Bovary without the opportunities', is how my mother puts it.

'Were you close to your mother?' I ask. 'Could you confide in her when you were little?'

'Not at all. She didn't have anything to do with us – except Peter whom she spoiled. My mother had no interest in girls. She couldn't be left alone with us for a minute. On Nanny's day off a Norland nurse arrived and took over until Nanny returned.' (It was the same for us when, as small children, we stayed with our grandmother. There was no Norland nurse, so on Nanny's day off, if she was late back for any reason, we put ourselves to bed. Amanda, aged four, once had to go to bed in her walking shoes because neither of us could undo the knotted laces.)

'You say your mother was bookish. Did she read to you at bedtime, the way you used to read to us?'

'No, never. Nanny did that. No, she had nothing to do with me until I was twelve or thirteen – books were the bond then. And clothes. She began to take a great interest in my appearance. When she bought my school uniform, had it made, rather – we had a visiting dressmaker one day a week at home – she chose beautiful materials. My blouses were made of something softer and finer than other people's. I had a lovely trousseau at school – not showy off, you understand, but stylish. I was always well-dressed even for prep.'

This is an eye-opener; I think about it while my mother goes on to talk of other aspects of her education. What she says about my grandmother's attitude to school clothes goes a long way to explain her own attitude when our turn came. Sarah, Amanda and I, all at the same senior school, were not dressed in the regulation uniform 'obtainable only from Debenhams'. Throughout our time at the place, my mother having decided the official gear did us no favours (we were fat), our shirts, tunics, maroon after-tea dresses (mine was royal blue), Sunday Harris tweed 'coat-and-skirts', even our gym knickers (grey instead of brown), were only vague approximations of the real thing, and acquired, often, from

some other department store – a waywardness that was particularly rough on Sarah when she became a 'captain' and
then Head Girl. School was hell anyway, and it was hard to
understand why we had to be put through the additional hell
of looking different morning, noon and night (provoking
sarcasm from the staff and gibes from our fellows), and for
reasons that had nothing to do with financial hardship. Now,
in the light of my mother's comments, I realise that in her day
'uniform' probably meant something a lot less fixed than it
did in ours; and that, if her actions were mistaken, her motives
were not unkind. No doubt she wanted for us the sartorial
individuality she herself had been allowed and revelled in.

'Best wishes to you both from Daddy. May you ever grow
more like your mother – I can't say fairer than that.'

The punning message on the greetings telegram to
Amanda and me on our Christening day, 24 August 1939, is
typical of my father. (The Second World War only ten days
away, he was presumably denied leave for the occasion,
receiving the blow, one suspects, with sighs of relief.) I still
have the telegram which has a picture on it, very thirties, of
spotted orchids peeping from a frilled box. Alas, Amanda
and I lived up neither to our father's hopes nor to the ideal
of lacy femininity implicit in the telegram's design. Our
mother was fair-skinned and slim and had corn-coloured
hair; she was pretty in a boyish, but not masculine, way. (My
father, playing cricket and catching sight of her in the crowd,
told his fellow batsman, 'That's the girl I'm going to marry.')
Amanda and I, dark-haired, dark-browed and dark-skinned –
so dark-skinned that peerers into our pram would ask: 'Are
they Indian? Or Negro?' – took after my father. He was a fat
man most of his life, known to his friends as Slim, and we
inherited his weight problem too. (Of other characteristics,
Sarah inherited his brains and low boredom threshold,

Amanda his wit and his temper, Henrietta his very blue eyes, and all of us, to some degree, his shyness.) He was an attractive man and women adored him; however, the sort of looks that suit a six-foot male can be disconcerting when applied to a small female child – two small female children in our case. It's clear from remarks made in the past, and from things she says in our 'interview', that my mother was disconcerted by her dusky and glowering twin daughters. (Although, she says, we made her laugh a lot. 'Your *bons mots* had Nanny and me in tucks.') She did not, as it were, recognise us. With one (fair) daughter already, she and my father were hoping for a boy, or failing that another Sarah. Instead they got the worst of all worlds, two unpretty, undainty girls who fought, and defended, each other like boys. My mother had to wait another twelve years for the one child with whom, in every way, she would be able to identify.

'Tell me about the war,' I say at some point in our interview (reminding her how the Anderson shelter in the garden always stank of pee because we used it as a lavatory); and my mother tells me again the stories about my twin and me we know so well. How one of us – she can't remember which – leaned from an upstairs window and shouted at the other in the garden: 'Come in, darlin' – the siren's gone, and they'll be bombin' yer head off!' (the warning followed up by shrieks of crazy laughter). How, the two of us in our double pram and having heard an explosive noise, one said authoritatively: 'Ah – a bomb', and the other: 'Don't be stupid, it's a motorbike.' About the war, as it affected her, she details the cold, the dark, the having to make-do-and-mend, the fish queue, the daily problem of finding enough – nourishing – things to feed three growing children; the loneliness, the fear, the lack of love and sex, the lack of any sort of fun, the aching, bloody dreariness of it all. I think (I've always thought) I understand how hard it must have been for her, a woman in her twenties, cosseted until now and *unprepared for the long littleness* of her war, stuck at home with us. (Although, with Nanny living in, and two nursery maids and a cleaner every daytime, she was luckier than most.) Had her circumstances been different she might have joined the WRNS, as her sister Caroline did, and put her energies into a war effort more to her taste than the unrewarding one of keeping the home fires burning on rationed coal. I like to think I have the imagination to grasp all this, but my mother says I don't and can't. 'You'll never know what it was like,' she says darkly. 'You'll never, never know.' Later, talking about something else entirely, she says: 'I've been in trouble all my life through being strong, from having a forceful personality. But if I hadn't been strong I shouldn't have got through the war.' I'm not sure exactly what she means by this, but it's true that photographs of her in the war years show her thin to the point of gaunt.

There's a sense in which my mother's war did not end when hostilities did in 1945. My father being a regular soldier, he didn't come home at demob time as many of her friends' husbands did. (Those of them that survived, that is.) Apart from the odd short leave, my parents were separated for nearly seven years, a strain on any marriage. It's not surprising they should have wanted to spend the time they did have together alone, without the encumbrance of small children (obstreperous children who were jealous of this stranger, their father; as he, I think, was jealous of us); and in September 1946 we were sent to boarding school, Sarah, aged ten, to a girls' school in Surrey, Amanda and I, just seven, to a coeducational prep school in Berkshire. The following year my mother joined my father in Washington DC, returning at the end of 1948 to take us back with her on the *Queen Mary* for a final five months in America.

'Was it difficult, being parted from us for a whole year?

Did you worry about us?' I ask my mother, and I remind her of the letters we wrote (and she kept) which say 'I miss you awfull much, do you miss me?' and 'Remember I can't live without letters when I'm at school' and 'Daddy, you've got to look after Mummy'. A year is an eternity when you're ten, or seven. These questions may not be quite fair, but I'm not asking them in order to punish her. At fifty-four I understand her reasons for going and can blame Hitler for it. (And anyway, compared to all those children evacuated in the war, sometimes abroad, some separated from their parents for five years – or never seeing them again – we got off lightly.) I'm asking out of curiosity, to learn how she felt, because we missed her so badly. The three of us worshipped her in those days.

My mother looks sad and is silent, thinking about it; then says: 'I suffered when I left, especially leaving Sally (Sarah). The expression on her face when I said goodbye nearly broke my heart. But when I got to Washington, no, I didn't worry. I knew you were in good hands. There was so much going on I had no time to be distraught, and it wouldn't have been fair if I had been, having made the decision. I had to blank you out. And then, after your father and I had had each other to ourselves for a while, we had fun planning a way for you to come out to join us. When we'd done that we really looked forward to it.'

And we really enjoyed it of course. Washington, and the Atlantic crossings to and from, was the high spot of our childhood. A few years ago I wrote a fictionalised account of our time there in a story called 'The American Dream'. My mother's read it, I believe; but I'm not certain what she thinks of it.

Twins, if they look alike, tend to get lumped together, their vices and virtues seen by outsiders as identical. ('The twins have done it!' was the accusing cry at school, and when one of us had not.) So, in search of a separate identity, I ask my mother how Amanda and I differed when we were small, hoping she'll tell me something new and wonderful, and not the character-condemning story I've heard so often of how, in our cots, Amanda would stand smiling with her arms outstretched, while I stood stiffly, arms straight down by my sides. What I learn is worse: that though Amanda had a violent temper ('She roared; I'd be terrified she'd never get her breath back'), I was invariably the one who made her lose it. 'You were cool and rather horrible, actually,' my mother says, adding, perhaps to cheer me up, 'You were the quicker learner, quicker at everything. You used to roll your eyes heavenwards, and I'd think "that one knows it all".' Which, if meant as a compliment, doesn't sound attractive. Another crime I've always been condemned for was for refusing to 'muck in' on family walks, for 'dragging miles behind, and looking at the ground'. Well, I shall retaliate here and tell about those walks: my mother, swinging her walking stick (the triangle of her headscarf in a dagger point) would march ahead, barking 'Heads up! Shoulders back!' – and even 'Tuck your tails in!' Occasionally this terrifying ATS sergeant would halt and point her stick. 'Look at that view!' she'd command her quaking troops. 'No, look at it properly – drink it in! Take deep, deep breaths!' I'd have gone AWOL if I'd dared.

My mother, a genuine enthusiast for what she terms the 'beauties of nature', is a talented watercolourist, particularly good at landscape and flower studies. She has painted all her life, exhibiting occasionally on an amateur basis although never showing her work professionally. The 'artistic' gene (there are painters in my father's background too) has come out strongly in her children – two of us paint for a living –

and her grandchildren, one of whom is a painter and several of whom work in art-related fields. Her youngest grandson, still at school, shows signs of being exceptionally gifted.

'Did you consider going to art school when you left the Mount?' I ask my mother, and she says no, life at home was too comfortable and easy, there was no urge. This reply accords with her answer to a question I put to her earlier about university and why she'd chosen not to go. (Unlike her twin daughters she was an all-rounder at school, good at games and gym – captain of tennis and hockey, in the cricket team; but very able too at academic subjects. She was in love with her English teacher, she told me, one Hope de Joannis Miller, daughter of the Moderator of the Church of Scotland; as she was a bit in love with the games mistress – no names, no pack drill here.)

'The school wanted me to go, but my mother just wanted me to have a social life, so it was never a solid option. I didn't see myself as a blue stocking anyway. There were no attractive, amusing people in my year going up to Oxbridge; the ones that did go bored me stiff.'

'How did you fill your days then, after you left school?'

'Oh, I played tennis on the court at home, and golf – even joined the local hockey club, would you believe.' (Much self-mocking laughter at this.) 'I rode, of course, went to a lot of parties . . . had lots of good-looking young men who took me out to dinner or dancing . . . wore lovely clothes. It was all I wanted; I loved my life, loved it. I was never bored.'

The life (the life of Riley; the life that's one long – action – holiday) that her answers conjure up makes me wriggle on my chair. The years she's speaking of are the early thirties: we're in the Great Depression! Only a half-hour's chauf-feured drive from the big house with the tennis court are the dole queues and black-brick slums of Liverpool. I want to bring them in, but don't. Perhaps what stops me is my mother's happiness reminiscing about what was, for her, a free-as-air and happy-as-a-sandboy time. Later, playing the tape back, I'm struck too by a candour that sees no need to apologise or explain, or even invent a worthier-sounding lifestyle. Her honesty in this makes me consider mine. Would I, would anyone, with no obvious vocation and with her luck – the luck of never needing to go out and earn your bread – have done differently? She did, at least, appreciate her life, knew she was lucky. Also, although I've no idea how many hands the sack factory employed, there were jobs for ten 'up at the big house', so my grandfather, you could say, was doing his bit in a recession. Something my mother, his favourite child, may well be proud of, if I chose to ask her.

Which raises again the problem of selection. It seemed only fair, having agreed to write about my mother, that she should have her say. Yet I realise I have all the power: the power to choose; the power to cut (and to cut in); even to quote her out of context – which I hope I haven't done. Reading this through, I find she comes across, in places, as frivolous, as more frivolous than she is. My fault or hers? She was a child who, at her primary school, Sandford School for *Ladies*, 'loved to-learn' (said with great emphasis); who sharpened her pencils every evening in anticipation of the following day. Once grown up, she never did a job for money, but has worked for charities – notably SSAFA and the Samaritans. She plays bridge, does *The Times* crossword (maybe not now; she used to do these things). She's always been a reader. Her bookshelves show her reading history and her tastes: biography and memoirs mostly; but also poetry, letters and *belles-lettres*, the English classics, Chekhov. Names on the spines include James Morris, Lillian Hellmann, David Cecil, the Sitwells (Osbert and Edith), all the Bloomsburys, Brendan Gill, Aldous and Elspeth Huxley, Auden, MacNeice, Eliot, Betjeman, the Mitfords, Waugh,

Kenneth and Alan Clark . . . No surprises here, perhaps –
nothing too dangerous or polemical. Except that it's a good
list. Many of her 'sort' don't read at all.

Predictable in many ways – asked her opinion of contem-
porary art (I know the answer, naturally, and only ask to get
a rise) she says: 'When I tell you I'm a Giles Auty fan,' (she
reads the *Spectator* 'cover to cover' every week)'you'll know
exactly what I think' – my mother can surprise me. The
recent elections in South Africa moved her 'to tears'. 'It's a
miracle,' she says, and 'I can't think why the whites weren't
murdered in their beds.' Again, I've always thought of her as
true-blue Conservative (she's taunted me for years for being
a 'lefty'), but when the subject crops up in our talk she
thumps the table: 'I think all politics stinks. I'm completely
disillusioned. I'm not a Conservative. No, I'm truly not. I'm
not anything. And as for Mr Ashdown . . . ! No, I'm nothing,
haven't a home to go to any more.'

'Do you have any regrets?' I ask my mother.

'Not having any great grandchildren – I wish they'd get on
with it! No, seriously, not sending Sal to university, not even
considering it, not making it possible for her to go. That was
very wrong. A crime. We just didn't think about it. I thought
she'd just want to get married, almost at once, as I did. It was
a terrible waste of a first class brain . . .' she tails off, looking
down.

'Do you believe in God?' I haven't asked her this for years
and can't remember what she said last time. I think I'm hoping for an affirmative, something to pin my feeble faith on,
and also for her. In the past five years Peter has died, and
Caroline; while her beloved sister Ginny, after three strokes,
is speechless and helpless in a nursing home. (She goes to
see her, finds it unbearable.)

'Well, I'm not sure. I'm not sure what God is. I believe in
good, certainly, in the power of good. Will that do?'

We stop soon after this (she's tired, and I've run out of tape) and have a whisky, weak one for me because I'm driving. Whisky's her favourite tipple, as it's mine. We talk about it on the telephone. 'I hope you've got a large drink; I have,' she'll say at six; or (later in the evening) 'Are you as squiffy as I think you are?'

My mother never wants any of us to go, but I have to: I've got a dog and cat to feed. At the door she hugs me as she always does, tells me to 'drive very, very carefully' as she always does, adding when I'm in the car, as she always does (the injunction harking back, I imagine, to when we were little and had to cross the road): 'Look both ways.'

TWELVE GOLD BANGLES

Margaret Busby

Twelve gold bangles, Indian-looking and finely crafted, my mother used to wear from as far back as I can remember. One day she gave me three of them, and my sister three, telling us we were to share the others between us when she died. I have been wearing my six for four years now, every day. I have developed the habit of fingering them absently when I am deep in thought: pausing at my computer keyboard as I struggle to write something, day-dreaming, musing about work done or still to do. Are these the moments when my subconscious turns to my mother for inspiration? I don't know. But I know that not a day can have passed when she has not been in my thoughts. Yet distilling these impressions into words, evaluating the emotional legacy she left me, seems an impossible task. Speaking with Maya Angelou recently about her plans to write a book about her mother, I identified with her feelings of trepidation and dread mixed with longing to place that irreplaceable relationship on record.

The memories slip away even as I try to pin them down, as if they shun the clarity of calculated scrutiny. Like the old snapshots and letters I turn to for help and inspiration, the emotional context has faded and only the semblance of factual evidence remains.

There are very few photographs showing me with my mother that date from my childhood. There are many more of us together taken comparatively recently, from my thirties to the time of her death in July 1991. Perhaps this is unsurprising, given that I attended school and university in England while for the most part she remained in Ghana with my father, working tirelessly to generate the income to pay for a British education for me and my older brother and sister from his rural medical practice. There were no suitable schools in 'the bush' where we lived, and if we were to have to go away to school, my parents wanted to give us the best, as they saw it.

It is strange to realise that I lived hardly more than a handful of years actually under the same roof as my mother. Having been sent to boarding school in England from an early age, my siblings and I accepted being away from home as normal – what did we have to compare it with? – spending most school vacations in holiday homes with a surrogate English family, one or two with an aunt in Paris. Thus my early relationship with my parents was conducted mostly by mail. My habit of hoarding all kinds of written material – books, cuttings from newspapers and magazines, letters – is one I took on from my father, and it is from a surviving collection of letters received throughout my school years that I glean in retrospect something of my mother's state of mind, which at the time it did not occur to me to consider. My father's letters were sparse and infrequent, exhorting us to study hard in the hasty doctor's handwriting that indicated always more pressing things on his mind. I did not know at the time that my parents were going through difficult times; the financial sacrifices they made in order to pay their children's school fees left no room for much indulgence in the lighter things of life. But my mother betrayed little of this in her letters, and almost single-handed she maintained our link of communication with home, enabling us to believe the perhaps incredible, that we remained a close family.

To our childish missives full of the trivia of schooldays she responded with gratifying interest; hers was the driving spirit behind the correspondence and it is a safe bet that for each letter I wrote, she wrote at least two. She took a close interest in the school activities we reported, remote as they must have seemed from a small African market town: 'Will you remember to post me a copy of your school magazine and also the school photograph? I am so looking forward to receiving them. Please don't forget, will you? I hope the school will have recovered from this flu epidemic before Speech Day, otherwise it might ruin everything.' She heaped congratulations on us for any modest scholastic triumph, treasured to her dying day the certificates we won for piano and dancing. Our birthdays were never forgotten: 'I am ordering your birthday cake from Godfrey's of Bexhill – would you like a sponge or fruit cake?' (In later life I tried to make my birthday special for her, since she had done the work on the day it commemorated.) She sent us splendid postage stamps that were the envy of our friends: 'Today is the first anniversary of Ghana's independence, and as you see from the stamp a new issue is out for a few weeks. Keep these on the envelope as they will have today's postmark and therefore will be valuable.'

She made sure we had new clothes regularly: 'During the

holidays I asked you to send me your measurements – you failed to do so, so I have had to guess more or less your measurements for the pinafore dresses. If they are too small I'm afraid the fault will be yours.' We never went short of pocket money: 'I am sending you £2 in four Postal Orders. You should spend 5/- a week . . . I do not want you to run up any unnecessary expenses where you are, and if you need anything, write and let me know.' With only passing reference – which I fear I may have treated with less significance than it warranted – to her own health or state of mind ('Sorry I have not written to you lately. I have been in bed for a week, and now I feel much better . . .'), she would worry about our minor ailments, trying vainly to offer long-distance diagnosis and advice.

Very occasionally the strain of keeping up a cheerful front despite her own hardships showed, and her letters became more serious and emotion-laden than usual, almost as if she were speaking to herself, reminding herself of the point of the exercise: 'It is always a joy to hear from you. Sorry we have not written to you for some time, but the struggle out here is getting more and more difficult and it takes all our time to be able to maintain you all in England . . . There is however one bright spot in the whole affair and that is the continued good work you all are doing and the money thus expended is not in vain.' In her decades-old letters, some of the anguish and deprivation she must have felt in relinquishing her children to a privileged education comes through with retrospective poignancy in the incidental questions about our appearance: 'How much weight have you put on, and have you grown taller?' 'Sorry your dress is a little too short – can you arrange to lengthen it yourself? How old are the girls in your form? I suppose you are still the youngest.' 'What is your hair like? Has it grown? I'm sure you are taking more care and combing it out well every day.'

Clearly we were sometimes remiss in matching the frequency of our epistolary responses to hers; no doubt our preoccupation with childhood trifles clouded an appreciation of the view from our parents' side, and if the mild reprimands this provoked did not register strongly at the time, now they fill me with remorse as I picture my mother waiting with avidly lonely anticipation for news of her offspring: 'We were a little disappointed that we did not receive any letters over the Christmas season; anyhow you are forgiven, and I am sure next Christmas you all will not be too busy enjoying yourselves to forget your parents. That is the time when family think most of each other.' But then we had scant awareness of how hard it must have been for her to chart our most formative years from a distance. Any initial homesickness we might have had no doubt soon made way for petty concerns about keeping up with our peers; and certainly we would have felt the separation more keenly had we not had each other.

It was important to my parents that the three of us – my brother, my sister and I – at first went to the same school. My mother sat up all night sewing name tapes to our uniforms before we went to a school in Arnside in the Lake District. It was small enough to have a homely, family atmosphere – so small, in fact, that before long it was forced to close as teachers outnumbered pupils; among the other children were two little girls and a boy whose mother was also Ghanaian, whose father was an English doctor in Accra. Out of place we might all have been in the Westmoreland of those days but to us, with no comparisons, it seemed perfectly natural (bar the weather – I remember being singularly unimpressed when someone woke me up one morning to witness my first snowfall, and cold has remained my enemy ever since).

It was during the search for a new school that our

difference began to show. Prospective headteachers told my mother, in explanation for not taking us: 'It's not that we would mind, you understand, but the parents of the other children . . .' Eventually my brother was settled in a school in Somerset while my sister and I were accepted by one in Sussex, the first Black girls there. That notwithstanding, it prided itself on being an international school, and we would surely have felt more acutely aware of being foreign as time progressed had we not acquired friends from around the world – Persia, Trinidad, Singapore, Bahrein, South Africa, Liberia, Nigeria. It was an indelible illustration of what home life had sketched out for us. Our adventure in education reinforced the lesson that the world is larger than one family, larger than one tribe, larger than one race, larger than one nation. At home we were always exposed to diverse influences – not simply because our own relatives are so scattered, in Africa, the Caribbean, Europe, America, but because of my parents' conviction that it is not origin or status or age that matter but character. Those who visited our home and sat down to meals with us might as easily be illustrious or lowly born, ministers or unemployed, children or elders. (So now it seems unremarkable to me, though apparently not to some others, that I count among my friends octogenarians and representatives of every generation below that.)

Sometimes my mother came to England and would rent a flat in London for our school holidays, which she strove to fill with special outings like visits to the ballet. The treasured occasions when we did return to Ghana for holidays were memorable family reunions in themselves, longed-for homecomings. (The one period I recall when being at home did not feel like a special treat was after I left school at the age of fifteen and spent a year in Ghana before returning to London University. Nevertheless, I wonder if I will ever be able to arrive at Accra airport and not unconsciously search the crowd for her welcoming smile.)

No doubt my mother's acceptance of – resignation to – the situation that separated her from her children was governed by her own background which mirrored ours in that she too was sent away from home in Ghana to school, at one time attending a Catholic convent in south London. An African in Britain in those days, the 1920s, would have been even more of a curiosity than it was three decades later, and she had stories to equal and surpass every one we could tell about school mates wondering whether the black of our skin rubbed off, enquiring how we could tell when we were dirty. In many respects her personal stand against the prejudice and xenophobia she encountered was exemplary and far more determined than I managed. Whereas she put her foot down and refused to be cast in the role of a slave in a school play, it did not occur to me that I could take a similar stand when I found myself in the same predicament. It was in adulthood that I asked her about those days, and I wished I had had the benefit of her experience earlier. Yet implicitly in the way she always dealt with the world, she passed on the lessons she had learned. Certainly a pride in ourselves and what we could achieve was imbued in us from an early age, but it was my mother's instinctive empowerment that gave us the tools to grow to maturity in an alien society (my father's schooling had been in the Caribbean where the problems he faced were less to do with race than with poverty).

Although she long outlived her three score and ten years and had for some months been receiving treatment for a heart condition, her death when it came in July 1991 seemed too sudden and unexpected. As I stood in the silent hospital room with my brother and sister gazing at her still form, it seemed that the three of us, all over forty, were suddenly children again, orphaned. It is said that only with the death of one's parents does one truly become an adult; for me, the realisation came gradually, and much later, that this was the moment we became the older generation. Maya Angelou spoke to me of her concept of a mother standing between oneself and whatever else there is. I recently told a similarly bereaved friend that for me, with my mother's death, I felt l had reached the head of some reluctant queue. 'Sometimes I feel like a motherless child', Maya said, was the song most expressive of the sorrow of the African-American slave.

My father had died over a decade before my mother, in the year of their fortieth wedding anniversary. His had always seemed the dominant presence in our nuclear family and even after he was gone his influence hung in a lasting manner over our lives. My mother mourned him deeply. They had been a devoted couple, although overt expression of emotion came awkwardly to my father; the one time I remember him saying he loved me was a few months before his last illness, and he had seemed to be unburdening himself at last. But while it would have been unconscionable for me to see him ever give way to tears, by contrast my mother experienced joy and despair in an open and tactile way. She had an additional grief to accommodate when, almost instantly and symbolically, her vision deteriorated to the extent that she was registered as partially blind, unable to read without the help of a powerful magnifying glass.

The loss of both her husband and her eyesight hit her hard, yet at the same time seemed to liberate in her more of the strength that had carried her through countless previous hardships. She became more outspoken, venturing forceful comments on politics where once she would have deferred to my father. She had always had the ability to be unforgiving towards anyone who threatened the well-being of her loved ones, but now she mostly vented her spleen on those public figures or political systems she saw as perpetuating injustice, whether Margaret Thatcher or the apartheid regime. She became addicted to news programmes on television and the radio, engaging anyone who was around to join in debate about the state of the world. I admit to avoiding such conversations on occasion, not because I disagreed with her opinions but because I had never before related to my mother on this level, not having taken her seriously as a politicised woman. It was my mistake, for in her upbringing was ample evidence that she would long have been sensitised to such issues. Her father, for instance, had been a delegate at the first Pan-African Conference held in London in 1900, and speeches he made there on South Africa were reported in *The Times*. How could I always have assumed that the political animal in my family was my father, that my views had been predominantly moulded by him?

My parents' life together was mostly lived in Ghana (formerly the Gold Coast), in West Africa, where my Caribbean-born father had settled in the late 1920s, one of the few professionals from the West Indies who went there in the first part of the century. After my mother's death I came across a batch of letters he had sent to her in the 1930s, some years before they married. (As I write these words, I marvel at my previous assumption that my habit of keeping old letters is solely a legacy from my father. And what motivated my mother to preserve these letters for half a century? I fantasise that she knew I would find them, that they were a deliberate bequest to me as the self-appointed archivist of the family.) From these letters he appears as something of a mentor, instilling in her the necessity for character-building, almost consciously moulding her into the wife he wanted her to be, the one that his first wife had failed to be. At the time my mother was studying midwifery in Scotland, and his letters are full of encouragement and didacticism, questions about her thoughts and deeds, an examination of her failings and weaknesses from the wisdom of his ten-year seniority: 'You pity yourself for your shortcomings and seek every means of escape except the right one – working hard on yourself . . . I hate forcing my ideas on to you. I have no power to regulate your thoughts, your ideals. I can only hope . . . I have always tried to be your friend, though never to the extent that I could think or pretend you were right when you were wrong. I have tried to be a practical friend and to help you where I thought you needed help . . . It is a bit of a pity that most women attach influence to the least important matters. It is always: How does he look? Is he a good lover? Does he say nice things? Never: Is he decent? Will he be my soul-mate? What can one expect when one glorifies the worst tendencies in man? Not permanent love, whatever else . . . You wish me happiness but I don't think myself I expect happiness . . . Life is one continuous whole, and for everyone is made up of moments of happiness and moments of unhappiness . . .'

Although corresponding letters from her are missing, from what he says it emerges that she accepted his guidance willingly, anxious to please him and live up to his high moral standards, standards that were to be instilled into his children. My father's letters showed his dogged pursuit of excellence, his dedication to work and his unswerving certainty about moral questions. My mother's absent replies can be gleaned from his responses, her youthful pliancy and her tolerance of his superior intellect being transformed into self-reliance and a determination to do better. Curiously, and paradoxically, in the scenario these letters reveal, I glimpse my own personality time and again in my parents' contrasting personalities.

My father commanded respect, was idealistic and cautious; my mother inspired love, was practical and a risk-taker.

Between the lines I read the formation of my mother's character, the seeds of the principles by which she came to live her life and raise her children. Her capacity for hard work meant that she not only managed the household, worked tirelessly alongside her husband in his clinic, but was also something of an enterprising businesswoman in her own right, succeeding not only in augmenting my father's earnings to make our school fees affordable but putting aside enough to buy land, building the house in Accra where my brother now lives.

I have a sepia photograph of her taken when she was in her twenties. Beautiful and poised, swathed softly by a huge ruched velvet collar, she must have been the toast of the town. She was strikingly stylish in her youth. Earning a 'European' salary – above-average for an African – and with as yet no dependants, she could afford to buy the best. Before marrying in her mid-thirties, she had led a life of relative independence, earning good money as a nursing sister, able to spend it how she chose. She enjoyed the luxury of dressing well, as she was later to strive to dress her children well; but her wages also benefited other members of her family. Her father, like her husband, had been born in the Caribbean and had had a family there before settling in Ghana at the turn of the century. One of her half-sisters, whom she had not yet met, lived in Bermuda struggling to make ends meet with five young children and an erring husband; my mother paid for her to take a holiday in New York, and subsequently brought the children to school in Britain. Selflessness in the cause of family was something both my parents subscribed to.

One day my mother apologised to me for a spanking she had once given me when I was very young. I was already in my twenties when she mentioned it; I had no recollection of the occasion, and as far as I can tell suffered no lasting ill effects. But evidently it had traumatised her, and that she had carried the anguish with her for so long touched me, gave me an understanding of how much she took to heart her responsibility for shaping her children's lives. In later years she sometimes talked of how painful it had been to part with us, confessing that, given the chance to rewrite history, she would not do it again; and, empathising with her regret, I feel something akin to shame not to able to reveal any psychological scars for my part (my sister, interestingly, has continued the pattern by sending her teenage son to school in Sussex while she remains in the Ivory Coast, and he enjoys in equal measures being away and being at home).

What does it say about the different perceptions of children and of adults that a mother who herself had first-hand experience of having to leave home in the name of education, and (like my sister) survived it well enough, was willing to let her own offspring follow suit, to their benefit, whatever the cost to her adult self? As children, my mother and I had both suffered separation from our parents; but whereas, for me, it was the first step in consolidating a closeness with my mother – with each letter I would re-image her, seeing a snapshot in my mind of her smartly turned out in a favourite tailored suit and neat hat – in her case, she once told me, after years apart she would not have recognised her own mother had she passed her in the street. Her father provided stern but remote guidance, and from one or two of his surviving letters I form the impression of a strict disciplinarian with little time for frivolities – in many ways, perhaps, like my own father. My parents' association seemed unknown to him, and it was the year after his death that they married. My mother often spoke glowingly of him, a man treated with reverence wherever he went; and then my father took his place as the important male figure in her life.

It was maybe only in the last decade of her life I felt I

really came to know her, in the years after my father died and I saw her on a one-to-one basis, without the mediation of his approval or disapproval. She had moved to London and was living with my brother. Often I would stay the night, but mostly we would speak daily on the telephone, her girl-ish voice belying her age, and I saw her whenever possible on Sundays. She came to rely on this routine and worried if for any reason I had to break it. Our relationship, in fact, seemed grounded in mutual worrying about each other – or rather, the need to avoid creating worries for one another. Much of the time, therefore, we read each other through things unsaid. I was not in the habit of discussing with her in detail my problems connected with work or personal rela-tionships, lest it added to the fretting I knew she already naturally did about me, her last-born. She was the person who might claim to know me best, yet ironically the person I came to confide in least about certain troubles. Precisely because she was so close to me I felt I had to guard against hurting her, knowing that whatever caused me pain would pain her too.

The perpetual worries I had on her account were to do with her health and happiness, the fact that I had never achieved enough financial security to give her all the fine things I would have liked to, the lifestyle of luxury I felt she deserved. I felt I had failed her, though she would deny it. Whatever disappointments she may have had along the way about my chosen path – that I had not undertaken a more secure profession, had not given her grandchildren – she subsumed in her obvious pride at what I did accomplish. Her love and support were unconditional and humbling.

The balance of responsibility between us shifted as she grew older: I felt like her protector. But actually it was more complex than that. I prized my independence, like any adult child who still has a living parent, but it was her existence that gave validity to many of the things I did. She was there to celebrate my achievements, to boast of them to her friends. Although it could sometimes be a source of embarrassment and irritation to me to hear her recounting my perceived glories, the fact that she did this also made them a reality. Once she said to me, 'I don't know what I would do if anything happened to you', and that warmed me as much as it chilled me.

Her last weeks in the hospital were a trial for us all. I am not proud of the fact that I caught myself wondering if she were exaggerating her discomfort and disability; my mother was stronger than this, my mother was not frail and needy, my mother could stand up to anyone and anything. Perhaps it was wishful thinking, a hope that she would wake up one day as strong and indomitable as ever. Times before she had been hospitalised while doctors adjusted her cocktail of medications, and always she had emerged her cheerful, resilient self. This time she seemed to lack the will to try to get better, seemed to regress to helplessness, even once asking me to clean her after a visit to the bathroom. Somehow, in that simple pathetic request the processes and elements of birth and death met, as I confronted my origins in her decline, faced the realisation that I was childless but mothering my mother. So when in a moment of rare self-pity she declared, 'I'm tired of living,' I refused to believe her and stemmed her words with platitudes.

She did appear to regather strength within days, and in the last bantering conversation I had with her she asked me to fetch her perfume from her handbag. I teased her that this was because the handsome young doctor was due to make his round, and she laughed her tinkling flirtatious laugh. Twenty-four hours later, she was dead. The nurse told us that she had suddenly said, 'I think I'm dying.' 'Nonsense,' was the nurse's reaction, as mine would have been, for she seemed as well as on any of her good days. There was no urgency. But then she did die, leaving me a long, long way from home.

Looking at her lying there in her short nightdress, not like an old woman, more like a young girl asleep, rosary in her hand, I remembered then, and I remember still, going to lie beside her on her bed in the heat of a Ghanaian afternoon, feeling the smooth coolness of her forearm against my cheek, toying idly with the twelve gold bangles on her wrist.

STILL WORKING ON IT

Harriet Walter

How do I describe a voice? I can enumerate its effects, sensations, but I cannot recreate the actual sound with written words. The problem is the same when I write about my mother. There is the mother in my mind and there is the real woman. I am in constant dialogue with the mother in my mind, but the real woman is as hard to describe as a voice.

Photographs help me to be objective. I see a tall, dashingly dressed, smiling woman, saved from cold elegance by a constant slight disarray. Though, initially, to some her manner bears the intimidating hallmark of upper-middle-class confidence, most people quickly succumb to her outward-going warmth and sense of the ridiculous.

Older snapshots have become entwined with memory.

Whether these recorded highlights of my life are typical or exceptional, they inform my memory forever. I remember a day because I have always known the photo of it. Recently I came across some family photographs I had never seen. It was like looking at a stranger. I suddenly had to accommodate new memories. Actual recall is swiftly eclipsed by the stories we all tell. There is what I remember happening, there is what I have always been told happened, and there is my adult interpretation of it all. How can I tell the truth?

I was a wet little brainbox as a child, a stay-at-home, a clinger round mummy's apron strings, afraid of the wind, the night, strange noises, strange food, you name it. This may only describe one short phase I went through, but it has acquired the permanence of most childhood memories, in the way that one sunny day becomes a seamless stretch of hot summers.

My mother always indulged my fears. Every whine was hearkened to, every tear dried, every ache soothed. All very natural you might say, all in the nature of the love affair between mother and infant, but somehow, in our case, that love affair went on too long, or maybe I was too susceptible, because we still have not quite accomplished that journey along the spectrum from Smother to Other, with Mother as the healthy resting point. The habit of mind set in early: I was dependent on my mother, and she needed my need.

I felt this co-dependence sealed us off from the rest of the family. We were a team against my father and older sister, of a clan distinct from the 'Walter' clan. We had Italian blood on our side, and were warm and sensitive; they were English and tough. Where did I get these clichés from?

Around the meal table, I often perceived my mother to be the hypersensitive victim of sneers and teasings. I smarted with her pain (real or imagined I don't know), and rushed to her defence. My sister sided with my father. Genuinely? Or in retaliation against our exclusiveness? Maybe both. He was cleverer, more 'fun'. I had a sneaky feeling their 'gang', the 'male' gang, was superior and harder to belong to, but I took a defiant pride in my loyalty to my mother, and in her calling me her 'fan'.

Where did I get the idea that she was under attack? Ours was not an unhappy family. There were days and years of comfortable safeness, with the usual excitements and disappointments of childhood. But my memory focuses on mealtimes, when we were all four together, and it remembers those (maybe only very few) worrying times, when no voices were raised, no plates thrown, but there was this chilliness, this putting-down, which made me writhe inside. Was I humourlessly over-reacting to some playful banter from my father, or was I tuned in to some real undercurrents of hostility which would eventually lead to divorce? (Or, horror of horrors, did my side-taking in some way help precipitate it?)

To say my mother engineered my dependency on her sounds too calculating, too desperate. Neither of these adjectives rings true when I think of her. Her power was gentle and authentic. If worry and nervousness came in my mother's milk, it had come from her mother's before her. Anxiety is the inherited disease to which my mother is also the cure. The strength and comfort she could and still can give were rooted in her own needs. She gave me the words she would have loved to have heard from her own mother, and which she seldom did. I suppose her own longing honed her empathetic imagination to a perfect accuracy. When I am most desperate, she always says exactly what I need to hear.

I am soothed but also saddened by this, as her wisdom bespeaks an intimate acquaintance with pain which she must have suffered alone. Who did she turn to as a child? And from whom did she learn her mothering?

From early days, she knew she did not like her mother and that she was supposed to. According to the family mythology, my grandmother was notoriously spoilt, the only daughter of an Italian aristocrat and a saint-like, long-suffering English gentlewoman. She was harsh, proud and beautiful, and married a straight-backed (though I suspect weak-spined) army officer, a great sportsman who rode, shot and played golf with the royals. My mother's hero-father left the family when she was ten, remarried and lived abroad until he died when she was twenty-two. My mother rarely saw him, but with her heart and soul she loved him, and never doubted that he loved her.

I ask her now, why did he leave, why did he make so little effort to see his son and only daughter? She does nothing so crude as to blame my grandmother, and mocks her own lack of questioning. 'One didn't ask. One just didn't. And I didn't want to know. I didn't want to hear anything against him.' As for her mothering skill, her openness, affection and tolerance, she claims to have learnt these from her saintly grandmother, and her adored old nanny.

We often talk as if our parents and older relatives are fixed in the universe, as if they themselves are not growing, changing individuals. I talk to my mother now, and she is broader minded than when I was a late teenager (the worst times), less fearful for me, good at letting go. Time has finally taught her that I can look after myself (though I myself suspect my independence is a sham, knowing as I do that while my mother lives, I have a safety net).

Since infancy I have looked extraordinarily like my mother. Maybe, having had one daughter who physically resembled my father and who seemed already to possess his self-sufficiency, she felt the need of a little clone of herself;

someone she could feed with the mother's love she had lacked, so she could literally love her*self* in a way my father couldn't. Maybe somewhere she sensed that my father would have liked a boy, and needed to protect me from him. Maybe she had wanted a boy and was guiltily over-compensating. I have toyed with endless hypotheses, but the fact that remains is that I became my mother's extended self, or at least that is how I consciously remember being thought of, and thinking of myself. I had my forays into father-wooing tomboyishness, won friends at school, and palled up with my sister, but I felt these acts somehow to be betrayals of my 'real self'. In the deepest part of my heart I was always 'Mummy's little girl'.

Then things changed. The love between my parents altered and was eventually cut off. At the time, my mother was coming up to the menopause and I was approaching puberty, a damaging moment in both our histories. When my mother was going through God knows what agonies of rejection, repeated history, or self-blame, she would occasionally lash out at me or, worse, go cold and ignore me, and I, not knowing what she was contending with, experienced for the first time the negative side of being so tuned in to someone's feelings while not understanding their source.

What in a more evolved mother–daughter relationship would have been seen as a mild rebuke, or a mother's rightful ownership of her private moods and desire to be alone, I experienced as the bewildering break from some law of the universe. Suddenly she was separate, a stranger. This period had the quality and atmosphere of a nightmare. It was a belated first realisation of our fundamental separateness, and my consequent aloneness in the world.

The eternal summer days of memory had abruptly ended, and the actual autumn and winter that covered the crisis of my parents' divorce was appropriately harsh. Or is it again a trick of my self-dramatising memory that I have an abiding vision of that time of bare black trees thrashed by howling winds, and cold darts of rain flaying my already tear-wet face as I went on lonely country walks at boarding school? It remains with me as an image, an image of my 'true' self, helpless and without props, in a Mother-less hell. It is how I imagine the world will be when she dies.

Both my parents worked hard to make the divorce and my father's actual leaving as bearable as possible. After he moved out, my mother took pains never to criticise him, or discourage my affection for him. She behaved in an exemplary and dignified way. The one 'fault' which I have since accused her of was her compulsion to keep everything from me during the build-up to the event. She explains that I was picking up on things which she did not herself consciously know; that my father's announcement that they must part came as a complete shock to her. According to her version, when I was sent home from school, suffering from unexplained anxiety and insomnia, the family doctor had advised her that I was of a particularly nervous disposition, and might tip over some brink if not carefully handled. This came dangerously near to a self-fulfilling prognosis, as I mentally filled the silence which my mother's well-meant, protective secrecy wrapped round me, and imagined an elaborate hell.

Father figures had never been a preoccupation with me, not consciously that is. That whole role (whatever it was) paled into insignificance next to my mother's all-embracing succour. However, two main points strike me about this period of my life. First, I became intensely religious. God was said to be a father after all, and mother-love had failed to protect me from catastrophe. Although spiritual love still felt maternal, there was some ideal combination of mother/father love that I yearned for. I missed my father's physical presence, and maybe deep down felt guilty about missing him, not wanting to hurt my mother, and longing for God was more permissible. Maybe my mother had felt something similar when her 'God-like' father left.

The second point is more complicated, and is to do with the messages I picked up from my mother about men, and from my father about women, and which I wrongly computed. One abiding image of my parents that I retain is of them standing close to one another, face-to-face, in the hallway of our London house. She sweeps forward to kiss him, he jerks his cheek away. Did this happen once or often? He didn't hate or abuse her, but the message I absorbed was that a man's space and privacy were sacrosanct, a kiss a hardwon and much-prized reward. 'Don't cling. Don't ask. Do not disturb.' I now know that my father was an extreme case of self-protectiveness, and that there is much in his history to excuse that and to redeem him. Infinitely polite, he was and still is charming, and great fun, but his politeness suffocated any personal questions before they were even mouthed. This made him an expert at the unspoken rule. One knew where one must not trespass and one never did.

With men in general, looking so like my mother and having so many of her mannerisms, I learnt how to flirt and was secure in my femininity, but with my own father I developed a separate character who was valued for a sort of jokiness and clever quippery, a running jumping boyishness. Long before my father left, I had developed different relationships with each parent. Two characters were emerging in me which seldom overlapped. Of the two, my father's Harriet was by far the least well established, and after kicking a bit at my mother for not being my father, shrank to a little corner reserved for him.

A curious result of this over-identification with my mother, and feebly rooted relationship with my father, was that when my father left us for another woman, I felt the rejection more in my mother's terms than in my own. That is to say I felt the rejection of the wife for the Other Woman rather than a child's resentment of an imposter mother. Mixed in with these feelings was what I now suspect was a mutual rejection of one another by my mother and me. Being so like her, I was a reminder of certain needy fearful qualities in her which my father had run from, while I was rejecting her example of femininity as having failed to keep her man, and maybe blamed her for creating in me a similar creature, who failed to keep my father's interest. The fact that I was not yet physically a woman when my father left further confused the message.

Once my father had gone, the family groupings were reshuffled. My mother started to lean on my sister, she was after all the eldest, although only sixteen. Stoically, privately (as was her habit) going through her own pain, which would surface much later in life, my sister became my mother's confidante. Also, because of her physical and in many ways temperamental similarity to my father, I feel in some way she became a surrogate husband. Returning from boarding school in the holidays, I sensed this alliance which had grown up between them, and felt excluded. My mother may have lavished extra care on me, seeing me as the helpless one, but this did not make me her favourite. She adored my sister equally but very differently, and now it was her turn. A new pattern had set in, which would last pretty well up to the present day: my sister was the adult, and I the eternal child.

Until this point, the younger I behaved the more maternal affection and protection I received. Now, all of a sudden, those qualities that had most endeared me to my mother no longer seemed valuable. She needed support of a kind I couldn't give, and which I felt she wouldn't accept from me.

Caring for her was the department of my sister and of the new man in my mother's life, who eventually became my stepfather. She was in fact coping with enormous difficulties which we have since discussed, but from which at the time she was determined to protect me. Feeling unnecessary, I wrapped myself in my self-centred resentment, and blunderingly tried to grow apart. I put my energy (though not too much trust) into school friends, work, and my budding interest in acting, very much the support system I rely on to this day.

I had started at a rather liberal, arty school where it was the fashion to vote Labour, hate games and love Virginia Woolf. I felt wonderfully at home. Then, during the holidays, I would have the blue-stocking stuffing knocked out of me, at the onset of the first childish tantrum to which my mother could so effortlessly reduce me. A fairly familiar teenage scenario really, but unfortunately it lasted well into my twenties and occasionally beyond!

However psychically and emotionally bonded to her, I was intellectually growing free of her. I belonged to a generation noted for its unprecedentedly dramatic break from parental values. For one thing, my mother and I had totally different female role models. She aspired to a Celia Johnson code of honour, and an Audrey Hepburn grace, while I was having my head turned (or confirmed in where it had always been without knowing it) by Germaine Greer. So our lives and value systems forked apart, but the apartness always pained me.

Having secrets from my mother felt threatening, as though, in developing privately away from her, I was not being true to my 'real' self. Screaming at full throttle I knew was not the way to convert her to my new-found socialism and feminism, but scream I did and I still don't quite understand why. Roughly from the ages of thirteen to thirty-five, I could barely conduct a normal conversation with my mother. I either grunted, whined or shrieked, struggling to resist her questions about my daily life, friendships, etc., while knowing that I would eventually voluntarily spill all the beans, kiss and make up. I felt poisoned by my 'unnatural' behaviour, and at the same time trapped in an almost physical inability to change it. I was desperate to gain her blessing to pursue the beliefs which in my view did not contradict the humanitarian values she had brought me up with; to fight against the male-imposed class barriers that I wished she could see beyond.

Why did I need her approval? Other friends of mine had made clean breaks with their parents, were even in some cases able to despise them, but for me a clean break would have been inappropriate and out of character. My mother had successfully inculcated in me the automatic fear/respect for authority and the *status quo* with which she had grown up. I was not a natural rebel, and under the glare of what I felt to be her X-ray vision, I squirmed with the unsureness of my new ground. So I battled on the hard way, determined to reconcile her, to reach a peace that might eventually release me from her benign but smothering blanket, from an emotional need that would leave me naked when she died.

Throughout these battles, I felt the anguish to be all on my side. My mother would be exhausted by me, but she resolutely held to her world view, dismissing mine as immature. She was seldom pathetic, but in our arguments I felt guilt at wearing her down, and at the same time a loneliness and resentment that she felt no torment like mine, only an exasperation with my 'bad behaviour'. She tolerated, forgave, occasionally put up a 'You have gone too far' signal, and never understood. It was always I who apologised.

We strengthen in the areas which give us confidence, in which we perform well. I gained my parents' respect through my acting career. Creating beautiful homes and bringing up interesting children are my mother's and sister's areas (and therefore not mine?). Both my parents had always been interested in the theatre, and with my mother it was a passion. Curiously, though, I had not been taken to the theatre very often as a child. They did not sow my interest. For the first six years of my career, when I was on the fringe and in political theatre, their parental loyalty overrode their discomfort with the subject matter, and they always came to my shows. But when I went 'legit' with Shakespeare and the national companies, I have to say it was the turning point towards mutual reconciliation with my mother. I felt free to accept her love of me as a person. Some of my fights had been about testing her unconditional love. I screamed at her because I could. Now I could believe I had earned approval in a walk of life that expressly dealt in revelation of innermost things, and where passions that were too unruly and destructive in the home could be legitimately contained.

There was another turning point. A single event, which I consciously stamped on my memory at the time. As I have indicated, it is a mystery to me where my mother got her loving nature from, having had such a cold non-relationship with her own mother, and no great reason for trusting her father. She never had a sister, but she has several lifelong female friends. One in particular was more of a surrogate sister than the rest, as she stayed with my mother's family for long stretches when her own parents were abroad. She was beautiful, dizzy, fragile and funny, and my mother adored her in the unconditional way that was her wont.

She married an American and went to live in Washington, and that is where my mother and I last saw her about eight years ago. She was lying in a nursery cot, a wizened foetal creature with a milky distant stare. She was in the last stages of Alzheimer's disease. I, who had often accused my mother of living in a protected narrow upper class, of knowing nothing of the real tragedies of the world's underclass, of swamping me and arresting my development in the name of love, etc., etc., now watched her as she stroked this woman's hand, laughing again at some hilarious occasion in their past, whispering with gentle loving tones into her friend's probably unremembering ears. I realised then that my mother had a gift of love, and it humbled me. I consciously vowed there and then to release her from blame and my resentment. If she had caused me pain, it was through too much love. Any criticism of her faults seemed petty when weighed against her fundamental goodness.

I was the one most consciously burdened by the emotional deadlock of our relations. Now it was I who consciously broke the habit. It still took some hard work and a few years of therapy to achieve it, and of course we still have rows, but I have reached a peace inside myself. I have stopped the futile attempt to fortify myself against her death. I will never be able to lose her, even when she is gone. She is roses, and London gardens, she is wartime movies, and Frank Sinatra songs, she is Italy and France, and China tea. She is soaked through everything I see. I look at my face in the mirror, at my mannerisms, the veins in my hands, and realise she will always be with me. I still need her, though life would be easier if I didn't. I may still resist her probings with monosyllabic evasions, but I always tell her everything in the end. In daily ways, she drives me up the wall, but in the things that matter she is my greatest and wisest support.

I often project on to my future by way of my mother's example. I look to where she is, further along the road ahead of me, and I am quite comforted. Physically we are so alike that I can pretty safely assume that I will age well like her, and retain a robust constitution. She has a genius for laughter and enjoyment which has kept her young behind the eyes, and I strive to nurture that capability in myself. But how to age childlessly – which is most likely though not yet definitely to be my future? That I cannot imagine through her. There the projection stops. I am not guaranteed the 'immortality' she can have through me. I am part of a pioneer generation of women who have had the choice whether or not to marry, have children, have careers. There are forfeits to be paid for this unprecedented freedom, and at times things get very confusing. My mother is learning something from me now, seems to respect my choices, and only worries about my happiness.

My mother encouraged my sister and me to be attractive to men. Physical attractiveness has always been important to her. Imitating her from an early age, I knew how to charm men, but then what? I had no confidence that I could deliver the goods, and due to embarrassment, or the generation gap, blame what you will, my mother and I rarely had conversations about sex. From her I learnt how to attract men, but not how to live with them, and with my father's example haunting me, I still have a terror of making demands on them. No matter that my mother herself has moved on from the woman she was when married to my father, and is in a marriage with my stepfather which could not be more different; unfortunately the messages I got as a child about marriage and men have been the most lasting legacy. I protect men from the 'invasion' of my feelings so they rarely know the 'real' me, and (this is hard to confess) while my mother lives I don't really need them to. It is a complicated issue, and I am still working on it, together with those other ingredients uniquely pertaining to my generation which are not my problem alone.

I used to think that only the birth of a child of my own could alter my perception of myself as a child in the world, my mother had 'done such a good job' on me; but now I recognise another part of her legacy. Through her I have always found it easy to trust and befriend women. I know how to ask for and get their help, and I finally realise that I have always known how to listen and give emotional support in return. So I *do* have some mothering skills after all. On that occasion, at her friend's bedside, I gave myself permission to love my mother unconditionally, and am prepared now for our roles eventually to be reversed.

Frida Blumenberg

LESSONS

Anne Leaton

It's a warm southwestern afternoon in Texas. She is standing next to an automobile I can't precisely identify, although it would clearly be a 1930s model. The car keys dangle from a slender hand. She is somewhat distracted, I always feel that, not questioning a fact which has been emotionally fixed for decades. She is focused upon a door in the high, rust-red wooden fence before us. I am focused upon her. She is beautiful to me: svelte and dark-haired, skin a warm, slightly olive tint, the fingers jingling the car keys long and thin, beautifully formed half-moons on the buffed nails. A scent of perfumed soap hangs in the air around her. She is wearing a dress which in memory is dark forest green, silken, so that things slide across it, fall away from it. I am at a little distance from her, it has always seemed (although my location is

inexact; it is as though I float above the scene like an angel).
Watching her. Locked into this.

In a while, the gate in the high, rust-red wooden fence
which surrounds the Yards and Roundhouse of the Santa Fe
Railroad in this small Texas town will open and my father
will emerge at the end of his work-day. We are there to greet
him, to carry him home. His wife, his only daughter (is my
younger brother yet among us? I cannot say; I am an age
indeterminate . . .).

It's all there, really, in this early inescapable image. Her
beauty. My adoration. The slight distance. The hint of
absence. The ambiguous role of a father dead at thirty-five.

So many images. So many fragments and shards of memory.
I wonder what she taught me and go obsessively over my
lessons; with occasional shock I discover, even now, some
new, implicit teaching from time out of mind. After her
death four years ago, I found among her things a bundle of
love letters from my father, written to her just before their
marriage in the autumn of 1924. He is visiting his West Texas
family one last time as a young unmarried man of twenty. He
writes letter after letter to her – not many miles down the
Santa Fe tracks to the Texas town where they both live –
begging for a word from her. Why don't you write? he says
again and again – and tell me you miss me, tell me you love
me . . .

One letter to every four or five of his, I gather. Some such
punitive ratio. And that one not gratifying to the young man.
I feel his dissatisfaction with her casual letters that detail the
usual round of amusements. Not what he wants to hear. But
she won't give him that. She was only sixteen, but she knew
how to withhold. From whom had she learned this? Who
had told her there was a certain power in this? Practise this,
it will be useful . . .

How impossible it is to write about one's mother without including in this onerous inspection one's grandmother, one's great grandmother, all the female forebears. Not that the fathers and grandfathers played no part. But the milk flowed from these breasts, in these comforting laps we sheltered to ingest the early lessons, for better or worse. The fathers and grandfathers toiled in the great city-sized Roundhouse of the Gulf Coast & Santa Fe to keep the train engines at their black-steel magnificence or sat grandly within the cabs of these same engines, driving them headlong into the steamy, mysterious night behind a huge, piercing headlamp that illuminated only the tracks ahead, not the darkness on either side. It's the mothers, grandmothers, great grandmothers who bring us news of the surrounding dark.

My mother was the only child of a man whose own mother was as cold and distant as the moon and whose father was – for this or other reasons – a drunk, the two occasionally meeting to produce nine offspring, and of a woman whose mother had been abandoned by her husband before the birth of the younger of her two daughters and whose whole life had been an exhaustion of poverty and bitterness. It would be hard to imagine a pair less schooled in love, less able to instruct others in its processes. There were, of course, apparent signs of affection: my grandmother was 'a rock', my mother always said – to anchor to in direst need; my thrifty grandfather always had dollars saved for an emergency.

One can not only anchor to a rock but crash against it, splintering one's tiny craft into a million pieces. And the giving of money is not the giving of love, although many people in the more developed capitalist countries suffer this confusion.

My grandmother was afraid of men all her life. How could she not be? They deceived and abandoned. They had their way with you and were off into the night, never to be seen again, leaving behind the fruit of their lust. Perhaps she was also afraid of my grandfather – and what is fear? I ask. And how is it manifested? But she had learned through the years to placate and appease, to conduct her married life in such a way that he would have no cause for displeasure. She was sixteen when she married him; he twenty-four, a man who had travelled a little – at least from South Carolina to Texas – who treated her always as though she were little more than a witless child.

Her main fantasy was rape. It lay in wait for every careless female, from every deceptively innocent male. That's what they did, these men. Best to lock the doors, to lock the doors *inside* the house, always to expect the worst, because men were like that. Beasts. Only one thing in mind. She taught me this by word and suggestion when she was already in middle age; how much abler, more potent a teacher would she have been in her youth, when my mother clung to her skirts, listening and vulnerable.

The realest of my grandmother's affective life was spent with her female friends, in afternoon visits over cake and coffee, playing rummy, drinking iced tea in breakfast nooks distant from whatever children she might have brought along. 'I'm going to see Bayne,' she would say – this was the period when women often referred to each other by their last names, like corporate executives in England. And off we would go. I would amuse myself on the front porch of Bayne's house, or play with a neighbouring child. But I was always aware that secrets were being passed among the women inside the house, that the laughter was special, and a good deal of it occasioned by the habits of men, resulting in that queer kind of thing I later learned to call 'schadenfreude'. That the pleasure of the day was unlike any other.

When my mother was widowed at thirty-two by her young husband's third heart attack, she had been sixteen years married, had given birth to a daughter and three years later a son, had gone, finally, to live with her husband and children in a house only a few blocks up the street from the one where she'd been born. Despite the Great Depression, life had not been altogether unkind. Her husband, father, and father-in-law all worked for the Santa Fe Railroad. The trains never stopped running, short of world's end. Work-weeks were shorter and pay packets lighter, but there was always work and money and hope for a better tomorrow. My mother roared through the twenties: she learned to smoke (Camel cigarettes at 39 mgs of tar!) and to drink (corn whiskey from a Mason jar, made in a little nearby town called Glen Rose by a man considered by all the other men to be hygienic and honest, whatever that might have meant in the circumstances of Prohibition); she became a champion bridge player in afternoon foursomes of women friends and evening foursomes which included husbands; she learned to cook, with the proper caustic spices, the small pink beans favoured by my father from a boyhood spent on a West Texas ranch among Mexican cowhands; she perfected her cornbread. There were parties, dancing, card-playing and gossip, most of it done with young men and women she'd known since childhood.

Then my father had a warning heart attack, followed by another not long after. These slowed him down enough for it to be noticed by his bosses in the great Roundhouse where he worked; they passed him over in the next round of promotions, thereby breaking anew his already broken heart. My father's father came over to the house one day to announce to his son why the railroad had not seen fit to advance him, despite his endless study and hard work. My mother – somehow fixed in this particular horror – painted the scene for me very graphically a number of times. She always finished the same way: he just turned his face to the wall and cried, she would say.

What lesson was I to learn from this image with recitation? That some parents are cruel – or simply indifferent, which amounts to the same thing? That my father was brave or else foolhardy, since – having reached the end of his road – he did not call it quits but, on the strange contrary, built a house and moved his family into it? That in the very midst of Life, and among the very young, Death *is?*

My father died before we had lived in this new house six months. And so my mother went back down the street to the house where she'd been born, to the mother and father she'd hardly left; became once more a child, with children of her own. She never left again. That was all over, marriage, childbirth, all the rest of it.

Oh, there were other men in her life. Of course there were. She was a young, good-looking, vivacious woman, with conspicuous charm and a sense of humour. She was, moreover, an easy manipulator of men, an accomplished, longtime flirt. She took a secretarial course and was ready for the war when it came along in the early forties. The US government was desperate for clerical assistance, never mind experience. She worked at army bases in Mineral Wells and San Antonio. It must have been like going away to school or camp (something she'd never done): frightening in a way, but wonderful fun.

Frequent weekends, she'd come home in her little black Ford two-seater to visit parents and children. I remember hiding once (when it came time for her to leave) in the space behind the front seat – nothing back there but uncarpeted metal floor and an upper ledge for packages – and hoping that nobody would notice I was missing until my mother and I reached the city limits of San Antonio. What bliss it would be! The two of us alone (except for her room-mate) for weeks, maybe months . . . But my grandmother noticed my absence and a search was made and I was extracted, gently, from the little Ford coupé and kissed goodbye and made to wait, pining and sullen, for another three or four weeks for sight of her. In these interims I thought of little else but her presence, her embrace, the silk of her skin, the cool, sweet smell of her, her movement through a room, through the world. I was not yet ten years old. I had already discovered what passion was like, although I had no name for it then. I had already discovered the pain of it.

She finally came home for good from the army bases, and we moved shortly thereafter some thirty miles north to a larger town. My grandfather was given command of a new diesel locomotive (and finally of the silvery Texas Chief). Mother went to work for a mammoth company called North American (no noun ever followed these adjectives), which manufactured aeroplanes. She began as a filing clerk, and in no time at all she was in charge of the files in a gargantuan department, with a number of clerks working under her supervision. She was always very adept at ordering people around and taking charge of matters. She had to get up in the middle of the night and drive for an hour and a half down ordinary, non-freeway roads through suburbs with red lights and traffic cops to get to North American by 7.30 a.m. These hours were not natural to her. She was a night person. She suffered from this distortion of her bio-rhythms, but through the war years she endured it. When the war was over (and North American closed its huge military doors), she had a wonderful work record to show prospective employers. She had been well paid – for the forties. But she had saved nothing. That wasn't her way. Like so many children with thrifty fathers, she was improvident. (Later in life, noticing the difficulties my mother sometimes encountered by living right up to the edge of whatever money she had, I came to take a little thought for the morrow.)

These are the men I remember in my mother's wartime life:

The younger brother of an old friend of hers from smaller-town days who was training pilots at a nearby airbase and came often to sit around on a blanket in the back yard on a Texas summer evening of heat and fireflies and faint south breezes. He had immensely bloodshot eyes, and I overheard my mother telling my grandmother how distressed the Lieutenant was by his duties: he taught men to fly fighter planes – and they went out and got themselves killed by the dozen. Was that the reason, I wondered, for the very red eyes? He and my mother went dancing at a roadhouse or out to eat huge, pink Gulf shrimp.

A rather prim gentleman who wore a metal neck brace which caused him to move his head and torso as though they were a solid unit; I was fascinated by this Monster-Movement. After they'd been out for barbecue or T-bone steaks, they sat in the front porch swing and chatted quietly, with occasional soft laughter, until my mother finally had to say goodnight, because even a young and healthy night-person required a little rest in those heady wartime days.

A tall, taciturn travelling salesman whose wife had died a couple of years earlier. He brought his drab daughter along on afternoon outings. She was about my younger brother's age, had tight yellow-brown curls and a face somehow the same colour. She was too subdued to play well (much like her father), but we put up with Wanda Zoe because Mother and Fred were 'going out'.

A burly, brown-haired, fun-loving fellow who took Mother

and my brother and me to every seafood café along the Galveston seawall on a soft afternoon of cloud shot with sun, gulls crying, and the constant wash of waves coming to shore. He enjoyed trying to catch the blades of slow-moving ceiling fans, which made us all laugh for some reason; perhaps we were drunk on that sweet, watery, summer air.

A big, broad-shouldered man whose moustache was undermined by a superfluity of suit cloth and hat. He appeared now and then (as a child, I had an uncertain grasp of interval) and took charge of things: my mother, for example; her children. I thought – with a mix of wonder, delight, and terrible apprehension: he's the one she's going to marry. He will say, You'll marry me, in the same way he said, First we'll go to Angelo's and eat. And she would.

But she didn't, after all. There was never to be another marriage – not in all those fifty-one years she lived after my father's death. Why was there not? A critical question, one I asked constantly from questing adolescence onwards. The explanation that was, explicitly or implicitly, continually suggested to me by my mother was that (a) having had the best (i.e. my father), she was not prepared to settle for less, and (b) her children – most especially her daughter – were not prepared to accept a defective surrogate father into the house.

I was confused by this because since elementary school I had prayed fervently in an unofficial way that a father of some presentable sort might enter this household. For many years I did not understand the rationale for this extraordinarily urgent desire. Finally, I came to see (years later, after an intensity of looking) that what I had wanted on some profound child's level was to deflect my mother's attention from me. A husband would have accomplished this. Would have turned that riveting spotlight of my mother's gaze away from a child made increasingly uneasy by it, yearning for an emotional privacy she was scarcely able to name. Because by this time she had come to realise that the early passion had created a closed door through which others could not enter.

It is possible, I learned, to be wholly in love with someone and on a mysterious level of consciousness be aware that one should withdraw a little distance, until light could be seen between these two bodies. And how extraordinary to perceive, coupled with this intense connection, a faint scent of absence in my mother, as though some little element in the middle of her heart had gone away, or never grown! How long does it take to learn to live with contradictions like these? Or perhaps learning to live with such contraries is exactly the process of maturing into the kind of ambivalence which allows one to abide the moral and emotional chiaroscuro of the human carnival.

After the war and a couple of desultory makeshift jobs, Mother went to work for a round, red-faced man who built highways. For the next twenty-odd years she managed his office and kept his books, more or less happily. There was no pension or retirement plan offered – or expected – in those days, not from an individual employer, but there were certain perks: gas for her Oldsmobile or (later on) her Ford, a generous bonus at Christmas, indefinite lunch hours, time off for family emergencies, a good deal of independence in the way she ran the office, and a little financial assistance when circumstances overwhelmed her, as occasionally they did.

A psychiatrist under whose care I later on came suggested to me that my mother's life and happiness were not, never had been, my responsibility. That this task (even if it could be accomplished by any one human for any other human – an entirely dubious proposition) was altogether too strenuous for an inexperienced child. No one had ever before suggested this to me; no one had ever before said to me in a casual, matter-of-fact way that this was the burden of my heart and the probable ruin of my life. It was a breathtaking turn of perspective.

Because, clearly, I had accepted that I was an impediment to her happiness. A tall, leggy, maladroit female child who always appeared at the wrong moment, demanding her attention just as she was intent on giving it to a suitor who would, it was suggested, have been, perhaps, a reasonably acceptable successor to the Ideal Husband she had experienced. Maybe even a moderately suitable father-substitute for her two children. But the thin, intense, adolescent daughter was unfriendly to these possible surrogates. Didn't want her mother's attention diverted, didn't like the thought of sharing her mother, didn't – in short – want her mother to marry. So the suitors fled before the Hostile Daughter.

And so, since it was my passion and possessiveness that ensured her unrewarding single state, mine was the duty to relieve the ill effects of this condition. Meet her for movies after work, for lunch at the hotel, for shopping, for visits to friends. Friend/lover/brief husband Willie said to me once – bemused (coming upon us in the street after we'd left one of these early evening movies) – 'You were like two sweethearts, I swear. Smiling at each other, holding hands, half-embracing . . .' And of course we were. I was the heir of the Perfect Husband. She need look no further for his successor.

All this began to change when I finished university and won my scholarship and prepared to go abroad. I knew this would not be a temporary farewell. I knew that something absolute was shattering: this ship which had carried me for two decades was breaking apart upon the rocks hidden beneath my waterline. Things would never be the same between us, I knew that. And she sensed it, too. She wept without restraint, that August morning in the fifties, as the SS *Gripsholm* drew slowly into New York harbour, bound for Germany. I had gone past tears into a fever of fear, anticipation, exhilaration.

When I returned from Berlin, I had erected a barrier which I did not allow her to breach. The old familiar intimacies were deliberately refused. I would not be drawn again into that suffocating room in which the two of us breathed each other's stale air.

I had also, in these intervening months, confirmed for myself what I had long known: that women were the heart of my emotional life – not men. From the university where I was doing graduate work, I wrote her a long, agonisingly difficult letter telling her what this revelation meant to me. Like coming out of the shadow at last, I remember writing. Like coming into the sun. When I came home from university for the Christmas holidays I learned that she had destroyed my letter, for fear that her own parents would, somehow, discover it. I was speechless with dismay. She had flung my heart into the fire. I never forgave her this betrayal, and she never realised there was anything to forgive.

So I learned something else, although it took a while for this seed to bloom: it is desperately hard for some of us to give up the comfort of being 'good children'. My mother was never to my knowledge able to confront her parents. She would privately resent; she would, within careful limits, openly complain; she would not confront. She would not, even on her children's behalf, become the 'bad child'.

In the following years the distance between us grew. She never quite knew why and never quite accepted that it had to be, trying now and then to revivify the old intimacies, insisting that the life between us was as it had always been. My tomorrows had no real meaning for her; she was captured by my yesterdays. Her bedrock connection was with a child-daughter who promised always to love her best, to someday build her a lovely house in which the two of them would live, happily alone. Somehow and on some elemental level she always expected me to keep the promises I had made her as a child.

Another clear, punishing lesson: one is never free of a passion which has entered one's child-body like a virus; this body never heals; this virus transmutes into chronic disease, sometimes called love. My mother remained a presence of great force in my life until she died – a force never wholly benign. We existed in an uneasy state of precarious balance: two emotional acrobats teetering on the high wire.

As children, we think of loss as a unique catastrophe. With age, we learn that life is a relentless succession of losses: friends, lovers, cousins and aunts, fathers and mothers. These blows are intolerable. We sustain them only to prevent losing ourselves as well. But each one is a wound that crusts into a red scab and ends as a white scar across the heart. Finally, our hearts become simply a white callus of scars where no blood can flow. And then we die, of loss. Perhaps there is no other cause of death.

I don't think I shall ever be able to erase from memory the sight of my mother propped in a wheelchair and left in the doorway of a hospital room, as though simply abandoned there. Her right side paralysed, one eye sightless, one side of her mouth twisted into a grimace, unable to speak; one arm lay bent in her lap, as though it remained where it had earlier fallen. It did not look to me like a real arm; it did not look to me like *her* arm. She was away, somewhere behind the eyes, deep in the caverns of herself. Travelling. Alone, the way she'd never travelled before. Her death scarcely two weeks later was merely an acknowledgement of this journey's end.

But this horrifying, persistent image will one day be driven out by one more real: on a warm southwestern afternoon she stands next to a 1930s-vintage automobile, not far from a high, rust-red fence. It is all there: her beauty. My adoration. The slight distance.

John Timbers

MOTHER AND CHILD

Sophie Parkin

'Taking this HRT I could be having another baby, now all the blood is flowing again.'

'Don't be ridiculous Mum, you're sixty-two.'

'What? I could. Don't be so ageist. We can go on having babies into our sixties now. The scientists say it's possible.'

'Yes, but would you want to? Besides you haven't had a fuck for five years.'

'I could do it artificial. It could be quite sweet to have a little baby about. What do you think, a brother or a sister?' she teases.

'Whichever you want to get up five times a night for, haul the nappies around and whose sick you want to wipe from your shoulder. I hear Mothercare's got a nice range of baby gates you might be interested in and there's the new school curriculum to study. Of course the Chelsea Arts Club doesn't allow children in, but you could get a nanny. It might curb your get-up-and-go travelling . . . but otherwise, why not?' I say, boringly and negatively practical.

'Maybe I've finished with all that, but it's a nice idea to toy with.'

'Toy with it and put it in the bin. And you can forget about me having another one to sate your cooing instincts. I've had my babies.'

'Don't be so selfish! Either you or your sister have got to have another one. The Guru in Rajistan said so.'

'Did he say *you* were going to have any more?'

'No, but he did say there was going to be another baby in the family. It could be any one of us.'

Mothering is a difficult subject.

My mother was brought up in a working-class Welsh family that moved to England to find that the gold paving stones were all grey. My grandfather apparently had violent rages when he would use my mother alternately as a punch-bag, then comfort-rag. He was a grand dreamer whose life could never live up to his wonderful imagination, full of jealous inconsistencies, and with an acerbic wit. He was a handsome drinker and a reckless gambler.

My granny was a neurotic, and a hospitalised manic depressive; an egotistical and vain woman with a soft, childish, coquettish tenderness. She couldn't face unpleasantness of any kind though she could be spiteful in drunkenness. She wallowed in morbidity, which wasn't so surprising having been the only one of her twelve brothers and sisters to survive past the age of five, but she had a glimmer of brightness that could light up like a sparkler and everything would change. Her mother, my great grandmother, was a small, wise and kind woman, a dispenser of sense to the whole valley; thoroughly religious. The times she and my great grandfather brought up my mother remain her happiest childhood memories, loving the mountain where they lived. My granny couldn't cope with her two children and would intermittently farm them off to her mother when things got too bad and the 'Nerve Home' called.

I never knew my grandfather, great grandfather or great grandmother so all I have gathered of them is hearsay from my mother, aunt and their village. My granny is now dead and my memories of her from my childhood sometimes contradict my mother's. Nevertheless they are mine just as my own experience, belief and gathered knowledge about my own mother and mothering is different from my sister's.

My mother always recounts the tale that the day I was born and she first looked into my face, her second daughter and last child, I seemed to have an aged wisdom beyond hers, had lived on this earth many times before and that I was much, much older than she was. Maybe this first impression explains many things about the way our relationship developed. She handed over the responsibility of the home to me and my sister when I was six, my sister barely nine. Perhaps she saw we were capable and ready for it. Whatever the reason, we were there more than she was, and we knew what we wanted to eat which was just as well because she was either never present or was on a simple diet of slimming pills.

It was the sixties and she says bringing us up in this manner was the way of the times, but I knew my class mates had different relationships with their parents, and their mothers were neither working nor divorced. Mum was working on *Nova* magazine as fashion editor and lived the extraordinary élite life of the successful in-crowd that came to epitomise London's Swinging Sixties. She was regaining her youth after she divorced my father when I was three. We had au pair girls who lived in, some nice some nasty, who looked after us. My mother seemed always to be working, un-availably busy during the week, so we had our front door keys on red ribbons around our necks and came and went just as we pleased from our house just off the Kings Road. That street of fashionable hippy decadence was our play-ground.

My mother was always there before putting us to bed, as she bathed and made herself up to go out, and at weekends. She never worried about household chores; she paid others to do those and I can't remember her ever nagging us about them. When she was there, when she was with us, it seemed that her role of 'Mother' was more as the provider of fun. Friends always loved coming over to our house because 'You can do whatever you like.' There were no stric-tures or rules.

We were her true friends, confidantes. The men in her life were always there on the perimeters, sneaking out of back doors so we wouldn't see them (that didn't fool us – they were passing and fleeting. She might have given them her time and bed space, but the love was with us, her children, and it was made clear to me that they never really stood a chance).

As her friends, she told us stories of the drunken débâcles of the night before. Tales of feckless or, worse, hopeless lovers who had failed to enamour, had us rolling about the carpet clutching our sides with laughter. We openly dis-cussed willy, wallet, fun and misery size. My mother taught me a brash honesty in all things – sex, Father Christmas and Easter Bunny. The fables of childish twaddle dispelled, I went straight off to school to ruin my friends' beliefs in storks and the mysteries of Christmas and babymaking with detailed diagrams and lurid descriptions.

'You see, it doesn't matter what size it is as long as you know what to do with it that counts,' I would say to cheer up the smaller-sized male members of my class who responded to my lectures with wide-eyed incomprehension. I got to know my mother's fallibilities and inconsistencies young. That's the problem with honesty – everything's on display, but then you don't have to lie or be eaten up with guilty secrets. Everything could be talked about, leaving me with just the rest of the world's views and prejudices to question. This kind of honesty and trust is rare and precious, and not all would advocate it for children, but for me it was what made our relationship special and able to accept all the other aspects of our life that weren't as perfect as I wanted them to be.

Maybe because of our responsibilities or of the trust put in us by our mother, my sister and I were never foolish or reckless and I trusted Mum as she trusted me. We were easy at making memories together; sitting in the garden, the sun on our heads, talking, always talking, having my hair brushed, plaited and pampered, drawing competitions around our big table, dancing in the rain down the street singing Hollywood musical numbers, eating faggots and peas in Cardiff Market, fish and chips on Brighton beach, picnics in Holland Park chasing squirrels and squawking peacocks or birthdays spent careering down the Thames at Maidenhead on boats we were all at a loss how to man-oeuvre through the locks. We were happiest just the three of us, I thought.

As a child, when you have had a sense of happiness, no mat-ter how often or how rarely it appears, even if there have been other nasty bits – from warring parents, drunken irrational behaviour, to school pressures – you imagine it will always be like this. The clouds are fleeting in front of a constant sun.

One day my mother fell in love with my stepfather and I suppose her priorities changed. It happens. I was now to be her ally with her for him, against him, to cushion him, mother him, respect and revere him. With that unquestioning mother-love, I tried to befriend and love him, to do as he asked and not to answer back. That was what she wanted, and what he expected.

The whole thing perplexed and confused me. Although I was quite happy to get along with whoever was put before me, the problem was with my understanding of the word love. Love is . . . what?

My mother loved me and never hit me.

My father loved me and never hit me.

Yet my mother loved, she said, and was utterly devoted to this man who regularly punched her teeth out, blacked her eyes and threw her about. She didn't complain, always had him back.

I felt that turning the other cheek had gone too far, many times. I hated him hitting her. It wrenched my insides out in a flood of fury listening late at night to the screams, the abuse, later the crying submissions. I couldn't respect him. Though I understand now that she often taunted him to do it, he wasn't man enough to restrain himself, and I hated him for that. I hated pretending the next morning that nothing had happened, that it had all been a silly misunderstanding to be quickly forgotten about. The honesty of previous years seemed to dissipate while the drinking escalated.

By the time I hit teenagehood and my hormones were whizzing about my body in an uncontrolled, manic state, the inevitable teenage revolt had entered my orbit. I became over-critical of my mother and her ideas on love, cynical of her lifestyle and relationships, sarcastic in conversation and probably impossible, with my cyclamen-pink hair and punk rant, to live with. Yet I still went to her for consolation, advice, wisdom and permission about boyfriends, contraception and whether to have my nose pierced. She always said 'Yes' but with tags of advice. To the last, 'You can always Polyfilla it in if the stream of winter snotty noses gets too much to bear.'

Thanks Mum. My nose remained unpierced, but it was my decision.

My mother was my friend, my eldest sister, my guardian and ally but drink, as with my granny, often turned her aggressive, resentful and competitive, down to fighting to finish the last bottle. Still, it was a shock around my eighteenth birthday to be shown the door and given a train ticket to London as though I was a fully fledged adult, wholly responsible for myself, when they moved to America. I no longer had a family home. I was eighteen after all. I envied the mothers that other students complained of when they went home to their old rooms with their starving bellies and dirty washing, to be mended, cleaned and fussed over before the start of a new term. I imagined these women as H.E. Bates caricature mothers, warm-breasted, sweet-breathed, cooing, concerned, hugging, soothing machines, a bottle of TCP in one hand to disinfect your pain and some calamine swiftly behind to soothe it. The kettle always boiled in the background of these pictures, for a nice cup of tea, a comfort cake or a crispy-topped macaroni cheese busy baking in the oven. No matter that they didn't understand your boyfriends, music or drug-taking.

When my mother came to London from New York on her fleeting visits, my reality was more Dynasty style, all shoulder-pads and a glossed, well-lipsticked mouth who kissed me with her cheekbone to avoid smudging and held me by my shoulders as a hug in some smart bar or restaurant. She couldn't stay long, there were interviews and photo sessions and dinners to fit into her packed schedule. Sometimes she would press a tenner or twenty into my vulnerably resentful, paint-smeared, art student hand, to get myself a decent jacket or at least have the one I wore dry cleaned. Often she brought me presents, the latest coloured make-up, see-through plastic handbags for girls who never carried tampons, and wild, rhinestone-studded strippers' stilettos to die for – to die in.

Now we were all adults behaving in a grown-up fashion. I was no longer somebody's baby or child, she was no longer a mother, we were individuals leading separate lives. I thought again, now it's like this it will always remain so, this is how adults behave, having sophisticated and distant conversations with parents, discussing other people's lives over drinks. During these years I would have surreal memories that didn't correspond with the truth before me. Pictures of us sitting scrunched up on Barry beach, Mummy recounting tales of her mountain childhood to our intrigued open little faces huddled warm in our woolly hats pulled down over our ears, and laughing. Always laughing. Mother and Child. My mummy, a bundle of warmth that secured us for the adventures that would appear on our horizons.

Things change, always, relationships, seasons, the tide. My mother, my self.

My mother's marriage ended, and she was bad. My granny died and Mum was devastated. She went through a terrible time but we were reunited through it and I stood there for her, a rock of a friend when others gave up. Her drinking and sexual promiscuity hit new heights or lows depending on how you view it. Sometimes she called me 'the Policeman' for trying to control her drunken behaviour, reprimanded for my prudishness. They were muddled times when I wasn't sure who was the mother, and I don't think she knew either. I would test her sometimes with parental duties that would prove too much for her and she would turn again to the bottle for her only real consolation. At last it got to the point that I couldn't bear any longer seeing this small woman grow to gargantuan heights of awfulness with each fresh drink, her mind and body unstable and choked with uncontrollable emotion.

When she said she was intending to marry a man I considered 'a real alcoholic' (your mother could never be one, she's just a heavy drinker), I took the easy way out and escaped on the first job offer going East, a plane trip at least twelve hours away. I thought that would be enough of a distance to separate us and to enable me to leave the misery behind. Unfortunately, whenever you travel with problems they have a nasty way of boarding your plane when you're not looking, caught up with the excitement of travel. It's only when you stop to unpack, have a moment of peace, they fly out to attack like a shoal of hungry piranhas. I missed my mum dreadfully out there in some men's idea of paradise. I longed for a windy wet afternoon, to sit in a cinema with her eating toffees or too much ice-cream. I missed her friendship, humour (there was nobody that I belly-ache laughed with more), and her love in whatever form.

I could survive being grown up, as mother and child to myself, but there wasn't as much fun in it.

When I finally returned from my travels, I was shocked to see her diminished state. She seemed to be a mask just barely standing. I wanted to help her, look after her, save her, but I knew I wasn't strong enough and she was the only one who could rescue herself, in the end. I let her go, believing in a happy ending. Somehow she would be all right, I prayed.

It was time for me to start my own family, have real babies that needed me, ones that I knew I could help to grow big and strong. I was four months pregnant when she rang me to say she was joining an alcoholics' self-help group. For two seconds I was shocked. An alcoholic to me was still a person who woke in the morning to kiss the neck of a whisky bottle. Not my mother, Mummy, Mum. Staying out for three days and three nights on one long drinking binge wasn't the same thing, was it? Sometimes she went for weeks without drinking. I was prepared to be wrong. I hid my feelings from her like so many times before when I deemed her to be too vulnerable, to protect her fragility. So I said, brave and strong as the daughter I thought she wanted me to be, 'I think that's a good idea if you think you have a problem there. They might be able to help.'

They helped and I thank them from the bottom of my heart for giving my mother the strength to live a different way. To regain her spiritual and moral values that had been lost for so long. For giving her a new understanding of her purpose in life. For letting her be Molly again and my mother.

Later she told me that the final spur to make her seek help for her drinking was the thought that I wouldn't have trusted her to be alone with the baby, her first grandchild, Paris. She was right, as always; the trust had gone, she could read my unease. She could sense my dread at the birth with her standing guard at the nearby pub, ominously called The Welsh Harp, however long the labour. I had already seen the scenario in my head of her bringing everyone from the pub with her to the maternity unit to greet the new arrival, my first born. Once Paris was born and she was there, sober at my side, I was able to joke about it, about the fears we unnecessarily build in our heads, but there was only a nervous laugh in reply, it was that close.

Four years into her sobriety, I left my partner and, with my two children, descended upon her. She provided a home for us all as a loving mother and granny. She even got a rocking chair, kept toffees in her pocket and was always ready to babysit. Our friendship was cemented by the year in that house which she had chosen for the fairytale garden and its proximity to the best school for my children. It gave her the chance to become a mother again and me a child to be looked after when I badly needed it.

Now we lead separate lives again and we can go to each other trustingly with problems or joys or for advice. We even go on holiday together as friends. At Christmas we went to India, the children left happy with their dad. We were free to return to mother and daughter, or just be easy as friends. We talked, cried and howled with laughter and always talked more. She unburdened her feelings of guilt that she had carried for so long and I was privileged to witness the unveiling of my mother's new-found acceptance of herself, as a mother, as a woman and as she was as a child.

Showing me her tortuous journey to witness and learn from, she had led me along the path of inner peace and spiritual contentment that I always knew would be there but would have taken longer to find without her encouragement. I can now pass this on to my daughter who is four, my son now seven, along with all the other good things she has taught me that I can happily see my children inherit as repeated family behaviour of friendship, fun and humour, leaving the destruction behind. I have that choice.

Recently a man friend said to me, 'So your mother's like your best friend. There's not going to be a chink of intimacy in any relationship you have with a man. You'll always share everything with her, won't you?'

'But I'll always need somebody to discuss her with,' I replied, laughing.

He was right. When you are a woman with a close relationship with your mother, who can compete? The comfort, the championing, the humour and familiarity, built for so long upon each other, is a hard game to beat. To trust an unknown quantity with a physical and emotional intimacy unknown outside childhood, you have to be brave. Far easier not to trust. But when you have a good and close relationship with your mother, it allows and encourages others. It's against suffocating exclusivity, it breeds belief and trust, it wants its child to grow kind, honest, strong, happy, graceful and independent.

I see my mother, sometimes complete as granny, Granny Moll. Loved and adored by my children whom she listens to and learns from as much as they do. Both of them consider her, 'Mad as a parrot. It's all that camomile tea you drink – you've got to stop,' they counsel her with their child's wisdom.

'Granny, I don't think you should move house, you've got a nice one already and you'd spend all your time doing it up and you'd only want to move again.'

Or, 'Granny, I'm worried about these new clothes you're wearing, I don't think you can wear them on TV because you might get the sack. People want to see you in your bright clothes, not looking like a mug of Horlicks.'

All cosy in her pale pure layered bundles, all the better to encompass my children upon her lap, in her arms, on her new matching sofa.

'Now you look like a snowflake upon the snow,' said Paris, my son.

I feel total love, trust, warmth and joy between us. The serenity she has now found after the turbulent life she'd led for so long is only what she deserves. It benefits us all.

'How lucky we are,' she said to me on Mother's Day surrounded by red, purple and orange tulips, 'that we've both reached this point so early on in life.'

'Yes, aren't we,' I said embracing her. 'Happy Mother's Day, Mum.'

Jane Bown

MAMA: MY INSPIRATION AND MY FRIEND

Carole Stone

We were together, in a London taxi, when it happened; just off shopping. Her last words were, 'Oh, darling, I feel dizzy. Do you know, I think I'm going to faint.' And she had a heart attack, just as she reached out and took my hand.

She died, as she had lived, with dignity and quite prepared to make that final journey. She'd always been ready to face life, tackling all that came her way with courage, compassion and hope.

Every memory I have of Mama is full of love. She taught me *how* to love – fully, but without dependence. And finally she taught me how to let go.

When I was born, my father had a milk round. My brother

115

Roger, born two years before, was already a difficult child – he was later to be diagnosed a paranoid schizophrenic – and Mama was running a village shop. Yet, despite all the worry about money and tension with Roger then and throughout my childhood, Mama made me grow up feeling I could do anything I put my mind to, and she made the world sound fun. It was with that feeling of optimism that I applied to join the BBC. I went on to produce its flagship radio series *Any Questions?* and to be on first-name terms with the likes of John Major, Esther Rantzen and John Mortimer. It was my mother's confidence in me that helped me do it. Luckily, a little of her attitude to life – her magic as I think of it – rubbed off on me.

She shared the ups and downs of my life, suffered with me and swelled with pride at my success or joy. But she never depended on me. Nor did she make the mistake of living her life through me. She was content to lead her very different life as best she could within the confines of her circumstances. She was a person interested in ideas, practical, cool and uncluttered by sentimentality. I was emotional and hot-headed. But we shared a closeness that never faltered. I can remember my slight sense of shock when I first came across someone who didn't get on with their mother.

Mama and I talked on the phone at least four or five times a week. When I was producing BBC's *Down Your Way* she listened to every programme and would ring immediately afterwards with her view. She would offer ideas for *Woman's Hour* when I produced the regional edition from Bristol once a month, and she came to the live broadcast of *Any Questions?* whenever it was near Southampton.

I loved her meeting the celebrities on the panel. She was never overwhelmed, just interested in what they had to say.

I can see her now, chatting to the veteran Labour MP Tony Benn about her own father who had been a member of the Fabian Society and paid his penny a week to Keir Hardy. And I remember when the film producer, Michael Winner, took her on to his film set. 'Just to be alongside your mother,' he said to me, 'makes you feel happy.' There's never been anyone I haven't wanted to meet her. She seemed to know when to be there and when to withdraw.

I have little recollection of my years as a child, except that my brother Roger was aggressive, pathologically shy, and demanded constant attention. My father, sixteen years older than Mama, never really understood Roger's illness, although he did try.

Mama had been born the eldest of three. Her mother, an ex-chorus girl, was highly strung and nervous. Her father, brought up in an Irish Catholic workhouse, had considered himself lucky to be apprenticed to a tailor at eleven.

She married Dada, an ex-Army boxer, when she was just twenty. They rented a small sweet shop and for Mama it meant exhaustingly long hours on her feet. To bring in a little extra money Dada took on the milk round, and in the evenings he liked to drink at the pub. Within a few years, by 1942, Roger and I had arrived, and Mama was blissfully content.

I remember her always busy. 'Ding' went the shop bell and she'd drop what she was doing – cooking, cleaning, answering Roger's endless tormented questions – push through the curtain separating our kitchen from the shop and serve the customer. And I remember her surrounded by books – she was always at the library and usually had at least two or three books on the go; she'd devour anything as long as it was non-fiction. Apart from the occasional Jane Austen, she was never really interested in fiction – she wanted to read about how real characters had lived their lives. My taste ran more to Georgette Heyer. I needed the happy endings of romantic fiction. I think it was easier to read and I lacked concentration.

Mama went to evening classes organised by the Workers' Educational Association whenever she could persuade Dada to look after the shop. She had a go at them all – philosophy, French, German, poetry, sketching, public speaking, trades unionism. She always said she was just good enough at things to be able to enjoy them. And that feeling, too, she's passed on to me. Mixing now in the world of politics and business, I'm on the fringe but understand just enough to find it fascinating.

She also taught me how important it is that, however great the pressure you are under, you have to keep a small part of yourself for yourself. That was how she coped. She was grounded and could stand alone.

She was an atheist, as was her father, but she had a spiritual quality – and a big heart. To her life was to be faced head on: 'Change what you can, but accept and make the best of what you can't.'

She loved Dada in a compassionate way – I don't think she was ever passionately in love – and she never wanted to change him. She just wanted to make him happy. She could never understand my agonising over men who made me cry. There was one who was as emotional as me, always sobbing (we both were). The relationship lasted about eighteen months. I say 'lasted'; I just hung on in there, crying and making up alternately. 'You're crying for what you hoped for from the relationship, darling,' Mama would say, 'not for what you've got.' How right she was. He left me, but Mama's common-sense advice had sunk in. On reflection, I realise she could probably have coped with him; seen him for the rather inadequate man he was and not expected too much from him. 'Never expect from people more than they can give, darling,' she'd say.

I often felt she'd had a tough life, a life looking after other people – her mother, her two husbands, her children – but she didn't see it that way. For her, 'if onlys' didn't exist.

She passed her Matric – twice, in two different towns, because Grandad was always on the move looking for work – and was offered a place at London University. But she couldn't accept it; she had to get a job as soon as possible. 'Oh, Mama,' I'd say, 'surely something could have been done, you would so have loved university life.' She would smile at my concern. 'If I'd gone to university,' she'd say, 'I'm sure I would have got a lot out of it, but instead I've enjoyed other things in life.'

By nature I'm just the opposite, more like my maternal Grandma, and I've had to work hard to learn to take things in my stride. My tendency was always to feel I might just miss 'The Big One' – the party that would put me in touch with Mr Right, or the phone call that would offer the job of a lifetime. But Mama taught me that if you miss one man or job, be sure there'll be others instead.

'It's what you make out of what life throws at you that matters.' I can hear her calm voice now. She must have been born wise. How I miss her.

I scraped into grammar school in Ashford, Kent, and got seven O levels. Then we moved to Southampton – Mama just shut her eyes, put a pin in the map, and that's the town she jabbed. She and Dada first took over a tobacco shop and then ran a newsagent's on a new council estate. I went to the local technical college for a year to get my secretarial qualifications.

I was born with a large nose, a coarse voice and big feet, but I was also born with Mama. Over the years her way of assuming that people would like her – her nose was just as big as mine – and would treat her as an equal became my own attitude to life.

I was shy, but loved being with people. I longed to be fashionably skinny and more confident. So at eighteen I went off to London to stay with my Uncle Bob (he worked for the Post Office) and my cousin Margaret in Tottenham, north London. For three months I worked by day as a temporary secretary, and in the evenings I went to the Lucy Clayton School of Grooming in Knightsbridge. This was the early sixties and I was mixing with society debs.

What fun I had! I was totally absorbed in the size of my stiletto heel protectors, the tightness of my roll-on and the shade of my latest lipstick. I was accepted as just another teenager setting out in life.

Mama had been right. And she wanted me to understand it too: rich or poor, clever or stupid, we all have the same worries. Are our boobs big enough? Will we ever keep a man? Meet people half-way and most will respond to you.

I left Lucy Clayton with top marks. I was thrilled until I learned we'd been marked on how much we'd improved and I'd evidently arrived at rock bottom! But that didn't matter. I could slip into a sports car without showing my knickers and the friendships I made there, although they didn't last beyond the course, gave me confidence to throw myself into any company.

Back in Southampton, just after my twenty-first birthday, I saw an advert for a news copy typist at the local BBC television studios. I wrote off, went for an interview, and got the job.

I was with the BBC! 'If you never do more than type and

make the tea,' Mama said, 'you're there, in an exciting world.' That was Mama. She never made me feel I had to set my sights high; the enjoyment was what mattered to her. But she made me feel I could achieve more if I chose to.

I left home at about this time and shared a flat with two girlfriends nearby. Roger was now suffering from chronic schizophrenia, and was in and out of hospital, often violent, whilst Dada was drinking a lot. The two of them often came to blows.

Mama managed. 'Take life by the scruff of the neck,' she'd say. 'You may not enjoy it all, but know you'll cope.' And cope she did.

I remember when she went away for only the second week's holiday she'd had all the time I was growing up. While she was abroad Dada died from a stroke. I met her at the airport with the news. She wasted no time feeling guilty about her holiday. She'd been advised to go to gain strength to deal with Dada's failing health and the continuing problem of Roger. She'd made the right decision at the time. 'That's all you can do, darling,' she'd say. She accepted Dada's death at once. Soon she was ready to look in a new direction. That was always her way. 'Do what you can at the time, then move on.'

It was that attitude that made me leave the BBC in 1990, after twenty-seven years. I still enjoyed producing *Any Questions?*, which I had done for the last ten years. But I was forty-eight and I wanted to try life outside the Corporation. 'Go for it,' said Mama. 'Even if you end up doing something less high powered. What does it matter? It'll be different.' She was all for testing your potential, finding out what you were capable of. All for experiment. That's what you can do when you're not afraid of failure.

I immediately moved from Bristol to London, added my

year's pay-off from the BBC to my capital, and bought a tiny flat in the heart of London. I was on my own.

I knew I wanted to have a go in front of camera – as a performer instead of a producer. I'd left the BBC with a bulging address book and I devised a series for morning television called *Mother of Mine* which would interview celebrities and their mothers about their relationships. It was accepted. I hit the phone persuading people like MP Ken Livingstone, Jeffrey Archer and Anne Diamond to take part. They did. I was in my element.

Those years growing up alongside Mama had paid off. I'd gained the confidence to know somehow I'd make a go of it and I felt sure I'd keep in touch with people. No pressure to succeed, just the desire to have a go.

Three years after Dada died Mama put an advert in the local paper for 'a lonely widower'. She knew she couldn't leave Roger and she had the shop to run, but she wanted to live life to the full within her limits. Ted answered her ad, and after three dates – all no more than cups of tea and chats – he proposed.

'Don't do it, Mama,' I said. 'You hardly know him. He could be impotent or a homosexual.'

'I like him, darling,' she said, 'I'll take that chance.' She did. They had thirteen happy years of marriage until Ted died in 1992. She'd been looking for adventure and she'd been ready to take a gamble.

Another thing Mama has taught me is how to adapt. In so many cases, it's your attitude that makes all the difference. I remember one evening just missing the train I needed to catch from Bristol for quite an important drinks party. I went back to my flat in a state of decline and inevitably rang Mama. 'You could certainly do with an early night,' she said. 'Take this opportunity to have one, instead of coming back from London as exhausted as you would have been.' She was spot on.

Roger moved into a council flat on his own when Mama remarried and she gave up the newsagent's. She went to live in Ted's home and adapted to a quiet life in the suburbs. She spent two days a week with Roger. They were difficult visits. He was usually moody and surly. Mostly he wanted Mama to drive him to a pub (he'd been banned from all those within walking distance) then more often than not he'd imagine someone in the bar was talking about him and would start a fight. Just occasionally all went well.

Then came Roger's death. Mama found him in his sitting room, having had a stroke. He was still breathing, half-sitting, half-lying in his armchair, surrounded, as always, by cigarette stubs and endless dirty cups – he drank tea by the potful. Mama rang the doctor and he was taken to hospital. He lived only four days, the last of them in a coma. He was a few days short of his forty-fifth birthday. Once again, as with Dada, Mama did not waste time on self-pity and guilt. 'If Roger had to be schizophrenic, then I'm so glad I was his mother and could look after him,' she said to me once.

She lived by what she'd taught me. She'd given Roger her devoted love, attention and help when he was alive. And now he was gone. She'd written a book about his life as a schizophrenic years earlier, *One in a Hundred.* It had helped her come to terms with his anguished existence, and now she set about coming to terms with his death. She felt the emptiness and the grief, but she made herself get on with her life with Ted.

When Ted died, several years later, Mama sold their house in Southampton and moved into my flat in Covent Garden. By then I was living with Richard Lindley, a television current affairs reporter. My flat had become my office, the base for my television work and the place where I held my lunches – most weeks I entertained around eight people – politicians, industrialists and media chums. So Mama had the flat to herself in the evening and overnight and was there with me when I was working; by then I had several consultancies advising companies on media matters.

The idea was for her to live in my flat for a short while until she'd found somewhere of her own within, say, a twenty or thirty mile radius. We loved it. We laughed and chatted and plotted. She joined in as many of my lunches as she wished.

But within weeks she went to the doctors because she could feel a large lump in her tummy. She was told it was a growth and that she'd have to have a hysterectomy, which she did. The growth turned out to have been cancerous, but we were told she was now fine. Obviously weak, and needing lots of rest, she was still determined to find her own home as soon as she felt stronger. Much as she loved living with me, she knew it was important for her to have her own base.

Within a couple of months she was progressing well and we started looking for flats in Richmond about ten miles away. We'd just decided to put in an offer for one when Mama's leg started giving her a great deal of pain. There seemed every chance it would have to be amputated.

Fifty years of smoking was catching up on her. She was told to give it up immediately, which she did, but she never again enjoyed a telephone call so much. In the past, as soon as she heard my voice, or her brother's or sister's, she would light a cigarette and settle down for a long chat.

She had a major operation which saved her leg, but her health was failing and we both knew it.

We had all those conversations that most women want to have with their mothers, but most never do. She was trying to prepare me for her death. 'Then these last few months will have been worth it, darling,' she said.

Once I said, 'Just give it to me one more time, Mama. If you were about to draw your last breath, what would you say to me?' She laughed. 'Carry on the journey, darling. Take in each new experience; keep on looking around that next corner.'

She was ready to go, yet still interested enough in what was going on to stay. As soon as she arrived in London she'd joined the Age Concern Club just up the road from me. Again she was sketching and writing and reading poetry, and enjoying it. And she was caught up in all my projects – and Richard's. But more and more often she just wanted to sleep. I was so happy that she let me do the giving for a change.

We never grew tired of being together. Her company was always the best. Her eyes still shone with pride and pleasure and excitement when I was telling her about something that I'd been doing. She was my Girl Friday when she felt well enough. 'Carole Stone's office,' she'd answer when the phone rang. 'Is that Carole's Mum?' would come the reply. She sounded like a calmer version of me.

Once I'd shown her the poet Philip Larkin's rather gloomy view of life and death in his poem *Aubade*. 'I'm an atheist, too,' said Mama, 'but that's not how I see it.' The next morning she gave me her scribbled reply to Larkin. At her service, in St-Martin-in-the-Fields, I read that reply. It ended: 'Your time was up . . . But not before you'd left your mark, and kindled for us a little spark . . .'

Mama's time was up on 17 July 1993. But she left more than a little spark. She left a blazing flame of courage, compassion and hope. I said at her funeral service, and I still feel it passionately, 'I'll do my best to keep that flame alive, so that my mother will inspire me in her death, as she always, always inspired me in her life.'

I wear her ring. I can still vividly picture it on her hand that final time I was with her. I kissed her forehead. She would be saying to me now, 'What we've shared together will always be with you, sweetheart.' And she'd be right.

I miss her all the time. Her voice, her smile, her love, her wisdom. But part of her has merged with me; I know what she'd think. She'd think: 'Go for it.' And she's given me the freedom to do just that.

John Hollingshead

AN ADVENTUROUS SPIRIT

Joanna Goldsworthy

When my second marriage ended, I decided to go to a psychotherapist to see if that would help. My mother was immediately suspicious. 'I suppose you're going to tell her what a dreadful mother I've been,' she said. At the time I thought it a peculiarly defensive thing to say (in any case, what had her mothering got to do with the state of my marriage?), if typical of her. 'The mother' (as my brothers and I used to call her) worked hard at the mothering job, and was sensitive to the slightest criticism. Now, with hindsight, I think I begin to understand what made her say this.

She was born, Margarete Hoffman, in 1917 in Blankenburg am Harz, Saxony, in what was until recently East Germany. Her mother, Eleanor, was English, her father, Ernst, an ex-army officer, Prussian. My mother recalls what seems to have been an idyllic childhood: tells how she and her older brother Hans-Jochen would go for walks with their parents and their two dachshunds, Seppel and Lumpel, in the Harz mountains where they spent their family holidays every year at the same small pension in the woods. They would play in the brooks, gather mushrooms, and catch sala-manders, lizards, frogs and even snakes for their terrarium at home.

Eleanor and Ernst ran a Berlitz School in Magdeburg, some two hours by train from the Harz, but language teach-ing wasn't a profitable enterprise in post-war 1920s Germany and the long hours in the school and the struggle to make ends meet took their toll on Eleanor who became ill with TB. Ernst, who by then had succumbed to his long-standing drink problem, was unable to cope, and Margarete and Hans-Jochen, aged twelve and fourteen, were sent to rela-tives in England while their mother went to a sanatorium in the mountains. When she died, no one thought to tell her children until after the funeral had been held.

My mother spent unhappy teenage years growing up in England. She had been called Daisy by her mother in Germany, but in England the name seemed to her a music hall joke, so at school she renamed herself Greta. She grew larger than her English cousins, felt herself unloved (hardly surprising she should think this; her impatient, careless aunt – photos show her at the wheel of an open car, hat rak-ishly askew – never visited her at school and on one occasion even forgot to arrange for her to be collected at the end of term), and had no real home.

Her father had more or less disappeared from the scene by this time; he had periodic bouts of alcoholism which inevitably led to being sacked from one job or another. On one memorable occasion, my then sixteen-year-old mother went to Germany to beg his employers – unsuccessfully – to keep him on. He died, early in the Second World War, having rejoined the army, but as with her own mother she only found out afterwards about his death (when a letter telling him of my birth, that she had sent through the Red Cross, was returned twelve months later), and it was some years before she was able to discover that he was buried in a cemetery in Holland.

In the mid 1930s my mother was sent to a smart London secretarial college (Mrs Hoster's in Grosvenor Place; I was also to go there some twenty-five years later) and before long had a job and a room in a boarding house. Here she met my father, a poetry-reading draughtsman, who took evening art classes and introduced her to the poetry of MacNeice, Auden and Isherwood. They were, as my mother never tired of telling me when I showed signs of conventional behaviour (which included wanting to get married), Bohemians, believing in free love, and freedom from bourgeois restrictions. Nevertheless, they were married in 1938.

I was a war baby, born in 1941, the first child of young parents. My father, by then a civil engineer, was engaged in 'the war effort', building a massive underground aero-engine factory amongst other things. Dependent on his meagre salary, my mother having given up work, we lived for a while in an old, cramped, wooden caravan on the top of a hill on the outskirts of London, but moved when nearby Biggin Hill aerodrome began to be bombed too regularly for comfort. We moved a lot; my father's job meant that we frequently had to pack up and travel on.

My brother Andy was born in 1944, and for a while we were a tight-knit little family, young parents with young children. One of the things that Andy and I enjoyed most was being told about our parents' childhoods. 'Tell us about the *olden* days,' we would beg. My mother would produce unsatisfyingly brief and in some way curiously truncated stories of her childhood in the Harz mountains and we would have to turn to my father for an inexhaustible – and more easily recognisable – fund of tales of his English country childhood.

Six years after the war ended, in 1951, my father was offered a job in Africa involving the construction of a water supply scheme on the Zambezi River in Southern Rhodesia. Britain was in the grip of post-war austerity, and this was too good an opportunity to miss. He flew ahead while my mother, Andy and I followed at a more leisurely pace on the Union Castle liner, the *Edinburgh Castle*, sailing down the west coast of Africa, and then by taking the famous Blue Train to Johannesburg where the three of us were to live for a while. My father met us there and then flew back to Southern Rhodesia, to his malaria and hippo-infested site on the Zambezi, thirty miles from the nearest habitation and quite unsuitable for the family.

This brief meeting was sufficient for my mother to fall pregnant again, and my most vivid memories of Johannesburg are of her eating dry crispbread and pickled cucumbers to ward off her nine-months-long morning sickness while I dictated stories from my children's books to refresh her shorthand skills. She needed a job; but all she was offered was the questionable one of housekeeper to a bachelor farmer on his ranch several hundred miles away. (Half-way there, rattling across the veld in his old pick-up, my mother got cold feet and insisted that the farmer turn round and drive us back to Johannesburg. 'Promise me you'll *never* tell your father about this,' she said to me; and to this day I never have.)

Finally Mum, Andy and I moved to Bulawayo in Southern Rhodesia; my father was still working on his job on the Zambezi, and would occasionally make the three-hundred-mile journey to see us. My mother had by this time learnt to drive (two lessons from a kind neighbour) and had bought a small car. Eight months pregnant, she decided one day to make an unannounced visit to my father. He was out when she arrived; no knowing when he'd be back, his servant told her – perhaps the next day, or the day after. She turned the car round and drove back. Falling asleep at the wheel, in the night in the middle of the African bush, she ran the car into an anthill, pushing the mudguard into the wheel. Somehow or other she got the car moving again. It amazes me the baby wasn't born there and then. (My mother was never one to think about consequences; spontaneous, bold and adventurous action with little forethought appealed to her – and still does. I've inherited a watered-down version of this trait, and have frequently got myself into trouble as a result.)

Six months later, we moved to Nairobi in Kenya. My mother had had the baby, a second son, and he was followed in rapid succession by two more boys. So I became the eldest of five children and the only girl, my three youngest brothers being between eleven and fourteen years younger than I was. I was little mother to these three boys, 'the babes' as Mum and I used to call them. I was nanny, surrogate mother, nagging elder sister, all rolled into one. No wonder I didn't want children when I got married! I needed to be an irresponsible teenager first.

My mother and I were like sisters, and it didn't surprise me when my boyfriends enjoyed her company. She was full of life, fun, energy; she was uninhibited, outrageous even. She drew these spotty youths out of themselves, would flirt with them and make them feel good. I didn't, consciously, mind this at all. After all, I was prettier and younger, and I never saw her as real competition.

But she was – and still is – a great tease. She likes to pry and to upset, make people (especially her own family) feel uncomfortable. She wants to love and be loved, to be noticed, to be the centre of attention. Gradually I retreated from her prying, was reluctant to share my thoughts with her. She was inclined to file my secrets away, to bring them out and make fun of them to all and sundry at unwelcome moments, leaving me floundering in an ocean of mortification. I wanted my own space, needed my vulnerable weaknesses to be my own.

I was helped in this by my parents leaving Africa, while I married – at the age of twenty – and went to Dar-es-Salaam with my husband. The marriage didn't last long; I fell in love with my married and much older boss, and left both East Africa and husband (boss stayed with wife) to live in London. By this time my parents had moved to West Africa with my three younger brothers, and I rarely saw them.

I remarried, and became even more secretive and detached from my mother, even though she was now once again living in England, and though I saw a lot of her. I'd married the wrong man, again (or more probably I was wrong to get married at all, to anyone), but I was damned if I was going to admit that to my mother. She persisted in her teasing and questioning, introducing me to acquaintances as her 'unnatural daughter' because I hadn't had children. (Little did she know – and I wouldn't have dreamed of telling her – that I'd been going through agonising fertility tests.)

I wonder, now, what it was that made me unable to communicate with my mother; indeed, makes me still. After all, I know, when the chips are down, she only wants what's best for me, has always been a 'good mother', is always there when I need her, is generous to a fault, concerned, caring, trying to be what she, herself, lost: the ideal mother.

At a certain point our roles reversed, and I became the protector, the stronger of the two. It happened when my eldest brother died of an undiagnosed brain abscess, causing my mother unimaginable anguish. A year later, another brother was involved in a motorbike accident and was severely brain damaged as a result, returning from a seven-months' coma to a diminished life. The effect on my mother was catastrophic; here was her family, so carefully and lovingly nurtured, laid waste. These tragedies took a terrible toll on her, and were it not for her indomitable spirit and inate optimism, she would not have survived.

It was hard to bear her pain while trying to cope with my own. These two brothers were, in effect, my own children, but to grieve for them was impossible while attempting to support my mother. And, once again, there seemed to be some sort of barrier to me sharing my feelings, my own agony, with her.

When she reads this ('You do talk a lot of *rot*,' she'll say, rolling the 'r' Germanically), she will know, probably for the first time, how I feel. She will realise how much I admire and love her, but how our shared history has contributed to a distance which isn't entirely to my liking. I would wish it otherwise! How I've envied those women who have remained close friends with their mothers, who don't face the constant challenges of supremacy, the emotional blackmail, the demands, the accusations.

Why is it that my mother is still unable to accept that I have ideas of my own, even if they don't concur with hers? Why must she compete with me on every level? Why does she envy me my career, my lifestyle, my freedom – my comparative youth? (And why, conversely, does she want me to be even younger still?) Why is the cloak my mother casts over me, to protect me perhaps, so suffocating, so restricting? Why must she control me?

These are unanswerable questions for me, ones that I have been grappling with for as long as I can remember. Of course I am now, at last, beginning to own up to the fact that

I am so like her, to acknowledge that all my adult life I have actively tried to be different. When my partner wants to annoy me, all he has to comment on is how like my mother I am. Instead of warming with a glow of pleasure, I can feel the irritation prickling through me.

What is ironic is that there is a great deal about her that I long to be able to emulate: her impatient fearlessness, her willingness to take risks, her disregard for convention, her energy. When, nearing their seventies, my parents returned to Africa, my mother plunged into a new career as a bilingual administrator with a German aid organisation. 'If you don't work, you atrophy,' is her opinion; keep working at all costs her motto – to the extent that when asked to produce official documents by her new employers, she changed her date of birth on her passport. And before long, she had managed to get my father a job with the same organisation. He wasn't going to be allowed to atrophy, either. Even now that they are, finally, retired, my mother keeps her hand in by doing translation work. And her adventurous spirit is undimmed: in constant severe pain from a deteriorating spine, and with a replaced hip, she drags my protesting father on cycling holidays in Provence, a place not known for its flat countryside. No, she will not go gentle.

My mother has grown into a beauty in her old age, leaving the homely ordinariness of her younger years behind. Appearance is important to her, and always has been. How often have I been given a beady-eyed once over on meeting her? How many times has the half-accusatory, half-admiring question been asked: 'What *are* you wearing now?' or 'What *have* you done to your hair?' (A placatory, 'Of course you're always so clever, unlike your dowdy old mum,' tacked on as she senses, with that sixth sense that only mothers have, my hackles rising.)

What I would like to think is that, before it's too late, my mother and I can recognise one another's right to be separate, can respect each other's identity; that we can rid ourselves of the need to control one another. We may be of the same blood, she and I, but perhaps we can allow ourselves to celebrate our freedom from one another. In the end, it is that freedom that will bring us together.

A SENSE OF THEATRE

Nina Bawden

d. Aug 2012
age 87

My mother was born in 1898. She died on Christmas Day, 1986, in hospital. We had seen her about an hour before and given her our presents. She smiled and thanked us and wished us all a happy Christmas. She held a necklace of ceramic beads close to her face; her hands moved slowly and her eyes looked greener than usual, larger and brighter, but somehow unseeing. Her cheeks had a heightened colour but the flesh seemed to have shrunk from her cheekbones since we had seen her the evening before.

We were due at my brother's house; he was cooking the turkey. I said, 'I wish you were having Christmas dinner with us, Mum, instead of in this mouldy old hospital,' and found myself choking on tears. She said, her voice sounding quite strong and cheerful, 'I shall enjoy thinking about you all but I am much more comfortable here.'

They telephoned from the hospital as my brother was carrying in the flaming pudding. A tumour in her lung had burst. She had been sitting in an armchair beside her bed, sipping a glass of Christmas wine – without much enthusiasm, I imagine; she only really liked sweet sherry – when she suddenly shouted, 'I'm finished.' She had always had a good sense of theatre.

She was just eighteen months short of ninety years old and suffering from a (mercifully mild) senile dementia. Until her last two years she had been a strong, independent and determined woman and it had been sad to watch her power diminish, her control over her own life slacken, fall away. When she died I felt sorrow and relief (for her sake) in equal measure. But, unexpectedly, I felt some anger, too. My mother knew I was cack-handed, my fingers all thumbs; how *unkind* of her to leave me to sew on my own buttons!

Figuratively speaking, of course. But to someone of my unathletic clumsiness, her physical competence had always been notable; not only the fact that in her mid seventies she could still turn a neat cart-wheel, but the way she could impose meticulous order on her surroundings. My son, Robert, said he would always remember his grandmother's useful, determined hands; making pastry, fastening double knots in shoe laces, unscrewing jam jar lids – to the end of her life she had stronger wrists than any other woman I have known. And the ferocious energy she brought to every task was fuelled with a kind of intense moral exertion. Even wrapping a brown paper parcel, she would seem to be engaged upon some larger, more significant enterprise. As little sighs or grunts of effort attended the tying of the string and the bold, black writing of the name and address, she gave the impression that she was not merely producing a miraculously neat and apparently indestructible item for posting, but celebrating the victory of the human spirit over the coarse, recalcitrant, material world.

I thought her quite fearless as well. I was afraid of so many things – the dentist, spiders, cows, barking dogs, angry people. My mother fed the fat spider that lived above the kitchen sink, tossing dead flies into its dusty web; in the country, when we stayed with my grandmother, she would walk through the field with the bull in it without once looking round to see if he was pawing the ground and tossing his horns; if anyone was angry she would shout back louder than they could. It seemed to me when I was young that she was brave because she was so sure that everything she did, or felt, was the right thing to do, or feel.

I wished I could be like her. Not just because she was so pretty, but because I was convinced that I was always in the wrong. If I was angry – and I was often angry, a tight, burning cylinder of rage – I clamped it down. I was once so angry with my mother that I stood on the narrow window ledge of my first floor bedroom, either intending to jump, or hoping to fall off, to make her sorry for whatever it was she had done or said to me, but when the sun went down and she didn't come, I came down from my satisfyingly dangerous perch and gazed in the mirror for a long time, admiring my sad, tearful face.

I think I may have been an unrewarding child. My mother once complained that when she came to meet me out of school, I ran straight past her with a surly growl, refusing to take her outstretched hand. In fact this was not a lack of affection on my part, as I fear she may have thought, but too much: I loved her so passionately that a dreadful shyness seized me when I saw her and it made me graceless.

I wrote her love poems. She had been born in May and I called her my 'Dear May Queen'. As I grew a little older, my love grew solicitous. My father was a marine engineer, away at sea so much of the time that he played only a very intermittent part in our family life. He came home with wonderful presents from the East, from Japan, from China, and we went to meet his ocean liner when it docked in Tilbury, but that was all. My mother had three children to bring up, an elderly mother to care for, and very little money. I didn't understand that until later, but I could see that she had no fun, no parties, no treats. By the time I was around ten, I had begun to be sorry for her, to long for something to happen to cheer her dull life. I read widely and eagerly and had happened upon Dornford Yates who wrote about rich and beautiful people who were always gadding off somewhere, a picnic of champagne and oysters in the boot of the Bentley or the Rolls. In other stories, mothers came to kiss their children goodnight in the nursery, smelling of scent and wearing fine silk frocks and sparkling jewels, dressed to dance the night away . . .

I ached with pity for my mother, dreaming of some handsome man turning up at the door to whisk her 'up West' for a shopping spree and a theatre. I bought her presents from Woolworth's in readiness, Evening in Paris perfume in a glamorous dark blue bottle. And once a most beautiful pale green powder puff from the hairdresser in the High Street. (I didn't have enough money to pay for it but I hung around until they let me have it cheap.) I scolded her for not taking better care of herself. I came home from school one day and her shoes were steaming in front of the fire. She said, 'I got caught in the rain,' and turned the shoes over to get the heat to the soles. There were holes the size of a penny. I said, 'You ought to get your shoes mended, you are so *lazy*.' She laughed and said, 'They are the only shoes I've got, silly girl.'

About this time, she had all her top teeth out. The dentist

we usually attended was a '1922 man' – it was not until 1922 that dentists had to be qualified – but on this occasion my mother went to the shabby surgery near the station where there was what was known as a 'Blood and Vulcanite' practice. She ate 'water toast' for tea that day – thick, white, buttered toast, softened with boiling water. I said, 'You look dreadful, just like an old witch. Why couldn't you have had stoppings in your teeth?' And she said, 'Fillings cost money, it's a drain, on and on. Cheaper to get them all out at once and be done with it.' And in fact, when she got her vulcanite teeth, she looked pretty again.

Having all her teeth out at once was a decision entirely in character, whether it was because it really was an economy, or because she was simply bored with having her teeth drilled. She had an impatient courage that not only met life head on, but made her go forward to meet it. 'If it's got to be it's got to be. Better sooner rather than later,' she cried many years later when it was clear she could not take care of herself any longer and a nursing home and professional care was inevitable. And, on many occasions throughout her life when some particular thing was obsessing her, 'I can't think about anything else until I've got it off my mind.'

She was the youngest of four children, her mother's late, last baby, her father's darling; a beautiful, fair child, thought to be delicate because she had nearly died of the scarlet fever, and so pampered by the whole family. She had an idyllic childhood in a country town in Norfolk and she told her children about it with wistful nostalgia; endless family stories about a poor but happy life in a cottage; tea laid on her mother's round, walnut table; a leaping fire in the grate around which the family pets, the jackdaw, the hen and the pig, took the best places.

The memory of this perfect childhood was very precious to her. There was no room in it for skeletons in the cupboard. Unfortunately, when I was writing *The Peppermint Pig*, a story for children about a pet pig called Johnnie who had a legendary place in my mother's family history, I talked to my uncle about *his* childhood memories which turned out to be grittier – less polished and sanitised – than my mother's.

My uncle told me about the old tramp he met one winter morning, sitting by the fire in the kitchen and shouting at his middle-aged aunts who were teachers at the local school to bring him a pair of new boots and 'a bit of belly pork' for his breakfast. This tramp, he discovered, was his own (and my mother's) grandfather. He had been a blacksmith who had taken to drink and then to the road, and from time to time, when he fancied new boots or a hot breakfast, turned up to harass his family.

I had written about a quarter of *The Peppermint Pig* when I consulted my uncle. Part of the plot (which was based on stories my mother and grandmother had told me) was giving me trouble. There seemed to be a mysterious hole in the middle. I seized on my uncle's old tramp and popped him in the hole where he fitted perfectly – the story falling into place around him as if he had been the missing piece of a jigsaw puzzle.

I was pleased with the book when it was finished and I hoped my mother would be pleased with it too: it was meant as a present for her, a daughterly tribute. Instead, to my astonishment, she exploded with anger. How dare I present her, at her age, with a dirty, filthy old tramp for a grandfather? And what would the rest of her respectable family think? Those who were dead would 'turn in their graves'. I pointed out that they had had to put up him with him when he was alive. And that, anyway, this was no sly fiction of mine, but something my uncle, her own *brother*, had told me. That made things worse. My mother didn't speak to me for over a year. When she did, finally, she hadn't 'forgiven' me. She had simply decided to ignore my treachery. When the book was serialised on television and my brother's small children chattered innocently about it in front of her, she pretended to be deaf. But she never spoke to my uncle again. She didn't deny that he had told me the truth. She simply thought he should have said nothing.

I try to put myself in her place. She said, among other things, that I had 'stolen and used her childhood'. I don't – and didn't – blame myself for that. All writers are thieves; theft is a necessary tool of the trade. She had persuaded herself that this was her story, not mine, and she should have written it. She had conveniently forgotten that she had encouraged me to write it, enthusiastically supplying details of her childhood at the turn of the century; the sweets she ate, the clothes she wore, the games she played. She had told me about the Harvest Fair where you could have a tooth pulled for sixpence with a brass band to drown your screams, about the old roadmender who sat at the side of the road with an axe and a pile of flints, about the dancing bear that came at Whitsuntide. She had even suggested that I talk to my aunts, to my uncle . . .

I told myself that it was just one of the hysterical outbursts to which she was given; great, windy rages blowing up (fairly regularly) out of a clear sky. But the depth and persistence of her anger this time suggested some deeper disagreement between us.

I was well into middle life when *The Peppermint Pig* caused her such distress; twice married, with three adult children. Years earlier, before the Second World War, when I was still in my first decade, she had said, 'Your trouble, Nina, is that you say things really *nice* people only think.'

This rebuke must have stung, or I would not have remembered it. But I cannot for the life of me recall what I had said that provoked it. Blurted out some uncomfortable observation, I dare say; it wasn't the first time I had been accused of 'saying things', and I knew I must have been at fault, even if I didn't understand why. Unlike my mother, I had no natural sense of propriety; if I thought I'd seen, understood, something interesting, I hastened to report my findings without thinking how they might be received. I once pointed out to my mother that she had been lucky, being the youngest child and having everyone doting on her; *my* position, as oldest, was harder, always having to give up my toys to my brothers, and not being allowed to sit on her lap any longer. And instead of laughing, as I had expected, she burst into tears and cried that she hadn't realised I was so unhappy.

I was meant to feel ashamed, I think now. At the time I just felt exasperated. All right, it hadn't been a very *good* joke, but it had been meant to be funny in a wry sort of way; suggesting that even if I did have a just complaint, it was only a mild one, not to be taken too seriously.

We didn't have the same sense of humour. Nor, more importantly, the same political views. My mother voted Conservative and was convinced (reading the *Daily Express* in the years before the war) that Hitler's plans for Europe were benign. Eleven years old, and in my first term at the grammar school, I was being taught history by a stalwart Fabian lady who intended her pupils to understand what was going on around them; history in the making, as well as in the past. In 1938 she spoke at length about the follies of appeasement.

I lectured my mother unceasingly. 'I suppose you are looking forward to seeing your little brothers blown to bits,' was her only response to my rendering of my history teacher's argument that the dark clouds were gathering and we should prepare for war. In reply I reproached her for taking an unthinking right-wing paper like the *Daily Express*, for voting for a party which cared nothing for the poor and the unemployed, for equating a Conservative vote with respectability.

My mother had a close friend who was a Labour Party member. When this friend stood up for me (very mildly suggesting that I might have some right on my side) my mother ordered her out of the house and, later, made her promise never to discuss politics with any of her children ever again, on pain of permanent banishment. When the war broke out and I was evacuated to South Wales with my school, our political quarrels were necessarily curtailed and, because of the war and the National government, were less passionate on my part. But I went on, throughout my teens and twenties, trying to convert her. Looking back it seems comic, the energy I put into this crusade. I think now it was another facet of my love for her. I wanted my mother to be perfect, which meant she must vote Labour.

I never succeeded in changing her political attitudes and at some point in my middle life, I gave up trying. Perhaps it was when we had the major explosion about *The Peppermint Pig* that I finally abandoned hope. Certainly, I think it was round about that time that I began to realise that good relations between us meant that I must make more effort to be 'tactful', and that grieved me. I thought that tact should come a long way behind honesty between people who were supposed to love each other. And why should it be *me* who had to show this tact, in any case? My mother had never shown the slightest inclination to mince her words to me, consider *my* feelings!

It seemed ridiculous, I thought – in my forties, in my fifties – to mind so much what one's mother thought or said. That I had been hurt in my twenties, when she was furious with me for leaving my first husband, was understandable. (Though what had I expected?) But to go on indefinitely hoping for her approval was unrealistic and perhaps a little childish. Not *grown up* anyway. The trouble may have been that I was in many ways so fortunate. My second marriage was a happy one. We travelled when we wanted to; we had help in the house; we might be overdrawn at the bank, but we were rich by my mother's standards. Although one of my two sons was schizophrenic (a diagnosis my mother characteristically interpreted as idleness and lack of character), our other children were well and healthy and successful. And then I wrote all these books! Did I expect her to praise me for them, too?

She, on the other hand, had stayed with my father; had never had 'another chance'. My father had been at sea all her young married life; she had brought up three children more or less alone. I don't think my mother was jealous of my luck, certainly not consciously, but it seemed to me sometimes that she thought the only thing truly worthy of admiration was misfortune. It was something you could get your teeth into, give you a chance to show your mettle. Any fool could have an easy life given health, money, a good marriage; death and disaster were the challenges needed to really build character! If you hadn't suffered, you 'didn't know you were born'.

Perhaps if I had made more of what troubles came my way in adult life, moaned and groaned and torn my hair occasionally, it would have done the trick; given me the right kind of moral advantage. But I would have been ashamed – and was probably incapable of complaining anyway. The war changed the balance of the relationship between us. In the term time, a succession of foster parents had taught me to keep my feelings tightly reined; living with strangers, on sufferance, does not encourage adolescent tantrums. And when I went home in the holidays – 'home' in wartime being a beautiful old farmhouse in Shropshire where my mother

146

was living with my two younger brothers – we were both too occupied with our new and engrossing life on the farm to want, or need, to quarrel or at least not in the conventionally competitive mother/daughter way.

My mother was happy in Shropshire; happier, perhaps, than she had been since her childhood. She had never liked living in a London suburb; life was dull and there was 'no air'. (I can remember her standing on the top of a Welsh mountain, arms akimbo, head thrown back, crying, 'Air, air, wonderful air.') She got on well with country people; with the farming family she was lodging with, who became our family too; with the postman; with the woman who ran the shop at the end of the lane; with the old Major and his wife who lived in the big house. She fed orphan lambs, reared a baby red squirrel whose nest my younger brother had shot out of its tree with his catapult, helped nurse the farmer's wife in her last illness. Her happiness infected me, made the holidays magical; I loved our valley, our farm, the bare hills of the Welsh Marches; fifty years on, it is still the place I long for, a place to visit in dreams.

When the war was over, my mother went back to London with my brothers and I was married in the autumn of 1945, after coming down from Oxford. Except for my holidays in Shropshire, my mother and I had not lived together after the war began in 1939, when I was just fourteen. I have no idea what difference that made to our feelings for each other. I know that from the moment I left home, my mother trusted me to look after myself; she never seemed to fret if I was late home or even didn't turn up the day I was expected. And because I didn't grow up with her, I may have remained somewhat childish in my responses to my mother, needing her approval as a little girl might do, wanting to change her political affiliation because I couldn't bear to acknowledge any fault in her, unconsciously (or deliberately?) provoking her by being flippant about serious matters – or matters she took seriously.

I know that until she grew old and dependent, and softer in her own approach to me, I was always cautious with her. I watch my daughter and eight-year-old granddaughter shout at each other with a happy, raucous freedom that I envy sometimes. I wonder if my daughter is more like my mother than she is like me, and my granddaughter more like me than she is like my daughter. There are some observable characteristics, certainly. My daughter is fairly sure that she is always right. She is obsessional like my mother. She likes to get things 'off her mind'. She is meticulous, organised; her house is always tidy. My granddaughter – both my grand-daughters – are untidy just like me.

The family dance provides a never-ending comedy. Fathers-and-daughters, mothers-and-sons, sisters-and-broth-ers, fathers-and-sons, any number of permutations. Change partners and you get a different story. I see my daughter more often than I see my son because she lives in London and he lives in Suffolk. Does that make us closer? My father was away at sea and so I know my mother better. But we are all mysteries to each other. My mother told me stories, about her childhood, about her mother, and, reaching back over almost ninety years of social change, brought the past out of the shadows so vividly to me that if I were to be set down, suddenly, in the Norfolk of the turn of the century, I think I might feel at home there. She brought the world alive for me with stories; that is a good gift for any writer, any daugh-ter, to acknowledge and remember.

A TRUE SURVIVOR

Julia Neuberger

My mother is a formidable character. Large, blonde, and blue-eyed, she was the very epitome of one of the Hitler *Mädchen*, but she was born Jewish. Life was hard for her in Germany before the war. Yet, unlike so many of her relatives and friends, she succeeded in getting out. A would-be commercial artist, whose entry to art college was made impossible by the Nuremberg laws, she went from Heilbronn-am-Neckar to Frankfurt, where she worked in a bookshop.

That was a staging post before leaving, though the bookshop owner became a lifelong friend, himself an illegal immigrant into Britain just before war broke out. My mother left, became a domestic servant in Birmingham, was helped by her employers, the Dobbs family, to go to the London School of Economics (which she never actually did), and to get her brother, ten years younger, out of Germany and into a school in Britain.

She never had a university education in the end. But she did succeed in getting her parents out of Germany too. Determined, desperate, she pleaded with everyone she knew to help her to 'guarantee' them by putting up the then not inconsiderable sum of £200 per head in advance so that they would not become a charge upon the state.

I cannot comfort my mother now for those she did not get out. As a child and younger woman, I used to get impatient with her tears. When, for instance, her mother – my grandmother – died in the early 1970s, she talked about that time. Her mother had been a difficult, mean-minded woman. Being a refugee had not helped to bring out whatever finer side there was in her character. Knowing the degree to which, for no good reason, my mother felt guilty about what had happened to her family, I still could not summon up the kindness to be gentle with her when her mother died. My grandmother had been a real trial to me, unlike my paternal grandmother whom I had adored. I had so loathed my mother's mother that the loss of her was almost a relief. I refused then to engage with my mother's complex feelings of loss, guilt, orphandom, and betrayal. My father had also disliked the woman intensely. For my mother, her family, normally to be relied upon in extreme circumstances to give love and succour more or less willingly on demand, had failed her. I am not sure she has forgiven us yet.

It was an odd business, her talking to me about her experiences as a refugee. It might have been easier if my father had been one too. But he was London born and bred, as I am, and in some sense part of that British establishment that could never let her in. Educated at public school and Cambridge, with parents who had themselves come from

Germany before the First World War for very different family and economic reasons, his life had been so unlike hers, and his grief at the holocaust so much more publicly expressed, and so much more resolved.

So who was she to talk to, this mother of mine, thirty-five when I was born five years after the war? Odd cousins were still popping up in her life who she had thought had perished: the brilliant young refugee electrician, her cousin Ernst, referred to as long as I remember as Ernstiboy; her second cousin, Ann Baer, who became close; her first cousin, the distinguished Hebraist and Arabist, Erwin Rosenthal, who became more important to her by his very survival. There were so few left out of a vast family.

For she looked back at a secure, large, lower-middle-class wine-dealing family, Jews who had mostly assimilated into the surrounding community. They thought of themselves as Germans. My mother, to annoy, still sometimes refers to Germany as the Fatherland. (It makes me wild.) Yet almost all of them disappeared. Their deaths had been unspeakable. She wanted, even needed, to recall them one by one. But it was never clear with whom she could safely and helpfully do so.

I was the obvious choice. I knew what had happened. My parents had never tried to shield me from the horrors of the extermination camps. Even now I shudder when my children's friends describe the perpetrator of some relatively petty unkindness as a Nazi. I knew what had happened. I was her hope for the future, her only child. Who but me should hear and understand?

Her attempts to engage me in listening were uncomfortable to a degree. I do not think she was aware she was trying to make me take part in this particular conversation. Nor was I aware that I was shying away. I must have been about eleven or twelve at the time she told me she wanted to talk to me about her family. By this time I was already dubious about how much I liked her mother, though I was very fond of her father. I felt exploited to some extent by having to visit them on the other side of London in the school holidays and performing menial tasks for them, things I would not have resented, would in fact have done with pleasure, had I been fonder of my grandmother. My grandfather by this time was beginning to develop Alzheimer's, and was apologising all the time for nothing in particular. I felt desperately sorry for him, but he was largely unreachable in conversation, though he did manage to have clearer passages of time when he would sing songs in the Schwaebisch dialect of German he remembered from his childhood.

But whatever I felt about my grandmother, I cannot excuse myself. I was old enough, or should have been, to recognise the fact that my mother needed to talk. She needed to express the agony of loss, the sense of endless wasted lives, countless achievements never made, of literally hundreds of her relatives. I would not let her. Like so many pre-adolescents, and indeed adolescents, I was self-absorbed. This was not what I wanted to talk about. The holocaust, and its effects, were her problem. She was, in my father's terms, 'bloody lucky' to have had as good a life as she did. She, after all, was the refugee. Why should I have to listen to her problems?

Now, having gone through that mid-thirties syndrome so often written about, of the child getting some sense, some relic, of that refugee feeling, and trying myself to express an unnamed and unnameable loss, I think I am beginning to know what it was she wanted to say. But she, of course, no longer wants or needs to say it. For she, too, is much older, and has talked to others, cousins and other refugee friends, rather than to me.

I should have listened. But I neither could nor would not. I now wonder why. Was it simply my age? Or the unbearable quality of her grief? Or seeing her in tears, as my children have seen me on many occasions? She often cried, my mother. She still does; we both have a large dose of un-focused sentimentality in us. But no other tears compare with that particular sadness, that desire to share with me what I refused to let her share. When I am generous to myself I say it was just my age. I was too young to take it in. But I suspect that I also did not want to. For there is no doubt that children can and do take in great horrors if they have to, or if they force themselves – though one might argue that they should not be put in that position – to be more mature than their years allow.

Mostly, my mother kept me younger than my years. I was loved, protected, kept safe. I used to rail at some of the restrictions. Didn't we all? 'But *why* can't I . . .?' It was my father's first illness in the mid 1960s which changed all that. Then, she began to rely on me much more. Having been unable to confide in me about her family in Germany, she did express – and I shared – her anxieties and fears about my father's health. We did not expect him to live to sixty. He was then in his early fifties. If we had been told he would be alive, though still with health problems, at eighty, at the time of writing this, we would have been frankly amazed. My mother began to paint the worst-case scenario for herself. He was going to die. She was going to be widowed. And I let her, even encouraged her, to do so. I believed, with a little cursory knowledge of half-baked Freud, that it was wiser to let it all hang out.

I think now it might have been better to be less accepting. It might have been preferable to tell the truth, which was that we simply did not know what was going to happen. But neither my mother nor I are any good at living with uncertainty. The certainty – completely wrong, as it turned out – we had created in our minds was that my father would not survive.

But survive he did, and for long enough for his illnesses to be part of the pattern of life for both my mother and myself, with our relationship changing over the years. She came to rely on me more, to trust my judgement on medical matters (though I am no doctor) and to want me to spend time with her when my father was ill in hospital, which became increasingly frequent. She was unable to be alone.

She still finds it very difficult to spend a night alone, though she rarely asks me now to stay with her and has wonderful friends who do so instead. It took years for me to make the connection with her refugee experience. She was frightened. She could not face being alone because of her fear. Her fears were different at different stages of her life, and they were often amorphous and unfocused. She was afraid of being alone, of my father's illness and ultimate death, of being widowed, of growing old. Impatience draws the response that we all grow old. My father will say to her that he sees no reason why she should be the exception to the rule that we all grow old and die. Yet he has not grasped, and neither of us has perhaps grasped properly, the degree to which she feels fear as a result of her ordeals as a young woman.

Those experiences may have been in Germany, at the hands of the Nazis. She rarely talks about what happened to her, about friends who did not speak to her, about those who cut her dead or taunted her. Or they may have been in the wake of discovering what happened to those whom she loved. Or they may have been the difficulties her parents encountered in coming to Britain, and her mother's unhappiness, and, later, her father's, as evidenced by what he said in his senile years – 'I am so sorry, I am so sorry . . .'

That fear is very real to her, whether it be of my father's death, of her own ageing, or whatever. She often says: 'It isn't much fun, growing old . . .' Of course, in many ways it is not much fun. One's body is weaker, and does less of what one tells it. One's friends die. One is able to do less. Yet outsiders see that she has a husband still alive, and friends everywhere, including friends much younger than she is. She has a daughter and grandchildren, whom she adores. She is close to her son-in-law, and likes to go to exhibitions with him. She has a rare zest for life, a passion for looking at things, for knowing what is going on. She needs to be involved, to see people, to hear the news. She has a magical attraction for young people who adore her enthusiasm and her eccentricity. Part of her can see all this, and celebrate it, but the other part looks on and says how much she loathes the ageing process.

Yet there is much to celebrate for my mother. She has, above all, survived. She survived both exile and refugee status, and the war. She became a proud British citizen, prouder than many born British. She has masses of friends and acquaintances. She is knowledgeable about art, and reviews exhibitions for a refugee journal. She reads voraciously. She sees her grandchildren. In many ways, it is a rich life.

Her very zest for life has been a deep influence on me. Although now she will comment on the degree to which my diary is crowded and my life packed with more and more events, it is *her* energy and *her* enthusiasm that has made me want to be so busy. Indeed, it is her sense now of not being as busy as she was, nor able to be, which makes her think about ageing.

But the question of survival is one that needs to be addressed. Is what makes her hate ageing so much simply the way she is treated? Does she wish doctors would accord her more respect, see the young woman inside the ageing body? Does she resent being told: 'But what can you expect at your age?' Or is it that the prospect of her own death, as well as my father's, is somehow Hitler's ultimate victory? She survived all that, only to be defeated by nature taking its course. Is survival so important, to someone who is one of so few survivors from such a large family, that to feel her own mortality creeping near is the ultimate insult?

Who knows? It is too complicated a thought ever to be confirmed or refuted. One never knows how honest one is being if one discusses these things, whether it is my mother gauging her own reactions or one of us trying to sift the truth from the rest. Life is not to be sorted into theories. Yet my mother would, I believe, have benefited from psychoanalysis earlier in life. She could not have afforded it then, and she is too old for it now. But it might have helped her to recognise some of the themes in her life, acknowledge where her greatest regrets lay, and make her easier on herself and on others, so that she could be calmer about ageing.

Not that I see her as one of Milton's Samson characters, in 'calm of mind, all passion spent'. I do not see her as the elderly lady portrayed by Vita Sackville-West in *All Passion Spent* either, her memories crowding back, taking a calm pleasure in it all. My mother is not calm. Everything is a big issue. She does not discard things as not worth bothering about. Nor does she ignore minor aches and pains. All discomforts, all inconveniences, are major ones. She loves life to the full and does not edit it, whereas the rest of us probably edit too much. Too many things are not worth bothering about, complaining about. We ignore the malignancy because it is only a small spot, and we do not wish to bother the doctor. We ignore the intense and frequent headaches because the doctor cannot do much about it anyway. And when there is a minor piece of news about our locality, we ignore that too, instead of drawing it to everyone else's attention.

In many ways my mother is the survivor *par excellence*. She is not going to be put down. She will be noticed, no matter what. She will make her mark wherever she is – and does so. She is not going to be a gentle and sweet old lady.

All credit to her for that, say I, though it is not always easy to live with. But the fact that she has such a tenacious grip on life, that she is so determined to get everything out of it, is admirable. For that reason, she is rarely depressed, though her exhaustion at looking after my father has made her more prone to depression than she ever used to be. She has mixed emotions about going away on holiday. She does not want to leave him, yet knows she needs a break. He does not require much physical care, but when she is with him, she always worries. The worry itself is exhausting, yet to go away is to admit defeat, and the idea of respite is not for survivors such as she is. That is for wimps, such as others. She can cope.

That strength is admirable, and infuriating. I think I have inherited it, as I have inherited her apparent certainty about things, of reasoning something through when there is no clear evidence. From her, I get my sense of 'just knowing' whether something is right or wrong. It is not easy to live with, for those who live with either of us.

Being my mother's daughter is no easy task, but it can be fun. She needs support more and more, but hates interference. She needs sympathy, but hates mush. She wants to be made a fuss of, but does not want us to be extravagant. It is not a winnable situation. Yet as I watch that immense energy and will to survive, I cannot fail to be impressed at her magnificent staying power, and by the fact that she has put up two fingers to Hitler and Nazism. She has not only survived.

She has done better than she would have if she had stayed in small-town bourgeois Germany. With all the sorrow, she has had opportunities, and taken them, and made something of her life. She is a true survivor, whose real regret is that she cannot be immortal.

Owen Bjornstad

THE WOMAN WITH THE FOUR FINE SONS

Gabrielle Donnelly

I was lunching alone in San Francisco, and eavesdropping on the next table's conversation. Two women, one older than the other, planning a party: they were talking in tones of mutual courtesy and respect, and each would allow the other to finish her sentence before she responded, pleasantly, with its logical sequitur. Co-workers? I wondered idly. Organisers of a charitable event? Different sides of a wedding?

When the younger requested more iced tea 'for my mother', I could feel my jaw, physically, dropping.

The first, and most positively the last, party that my own mother and I ever gave together, was my twenty-first. The fights started a month before the event; for thirty-six hours preceding it, we did not address each other at all; on the lunchtime of the day, I quite deliberately threw a plate of fish and chips at a passing brother, while she screamed across the house to my father a terrible and tragic family secret, of which I had had no idea, and which I delightedly hoarded to my bosom, specifically to fling back at her at some later date, with the accusing addendum, 'and *that's* what I heard on my twenty-first birthday!' The party, as it turned out, was more than successful. But, for the remaining thirteen and a half years of my mother's life, it never once occurred to anyone to suggest we might have another.

Listening to those two polite women in that sunny restaurant, overlooking the blue bay to the hills of Marin county beyond, I missed my mother. I missed her most painfully.

My mother. Mrs Donnelly, the woman with all the sons. Mummy. Herself.

She was born Mary Josephine Barrett, in London in 1921 (it was an excellent year, she would perfectly seriously assure us), the fifth and youngest child of Joseph Barrett, a dirt-poor London Irishman made very good indeed, and his wife, Alice Kitchen, who, to the horror of the entire Barrett clan, was a no-nonsense, non-Catholic, northern Englishwoman. The reaction of the Kitchen family to the Barretts is unrecorded. Mary was a pretty little girl, and charming, a classic spoiled youngest, beloved by all, forgiven much, demanded of little. When she was thirteen, her father died, her adored eldest brother, Tony, left home to be a Jesuit, and she herself was sent to boarding school at the other end of the country, a tragedy she never recovered from, and with whose dolorous recounting over the years I grew – perhaps unfairly – consistently less sympathetic. But the photographs of her at the monstrous Dothegirls Hall she created in her memory show nothing more Gothic than a laughing teenager, surrounded by friends, and swinging a tennis racquet; and when she went home for holidays, there, as often as not, would be Tony, visiting with his Jesuit novitiate buddies, the cream of English Catholicism's sophisticated young men, all more than eager for the chance of a harmless flirtation with pretty Miss Barrett. There are, to this day, elderly Jesuits dotted around Britain and Italy, to whose eyes her name can bring a wintry gleam.

After school came the war and the WAAF, a rather larky job in the Met office, a becoming uniform, and American airmen, instead of Jesuits, to flirt with. Stationed in Oxfordshire, she found herself one evening standing at a bus stop next to a handsome, dark-haired young navigator she recognised as Pat Donnelly, a member of her family's parish in London, and youngest brother, indeed, of Tony's friend Bernard. In 1949, when Pat had established himself in sufficient financial comfort to take care of a family, he and Mary were married at Our Lady of Muswell church in Muswell Hill, London. Eleven months later, the first of her five children, my brother Brendan, was born, and my mother moved into the role that had been awaiting her for all her life. That of matriarch. That of Herself.

There was no one like my mother. She was different from the other mothers in our quiet north London suburb, with their mild manners and well-scrubbed kitchens; no, Herself was something else, an oil painting to their delicate water-colours, an indifferent cook and impressively terrible housekeeper, who read to us instead of washing our clothes, talked politics and religion with us, watched the television news at noon, and 6.00, and 9.00, and 10.00, drank a bottle of Guinness every morning, and would not know a handy household hint if it knocked on the door and asked her to join the Jehovah's Witnesses ('No, thank you, we're Catholic'). In a good mood, she was a delight; warm, kind, and hilariously funny. She would imitate family members or actors on television, quote long and soulfully from *Poems of Today*, tell lengthy, engrossing anecdotes – complete with gestures, sound effects, and perfectly timed dramatic pauses – which even occasionally bore a glancing relationship to what had actually happened. ('Did she *really* say that, Mummy?' A withering glance. 'Well, if she didn't, she should have.') In summer, she would move wholesale into the garden and spend all day on the garden bench, squinting blissfully into the sun, and talking about Spain; sometimes, she would lift one leg diagonally into the air and announce that she'd love to be a dancer on the Val Doonican show. God, on a good day, my mother was fun.

All days, unfortunately, were not good. She suffered from depressions; she suffered badly – as I do – from Seasonal Affective Disorder, and when the winter came, she would take the cold personally, shuffling through the house in a motley of old sweaters, shawls, and mysterious garments that defied description, her shoulders hunched above her head, her grey-blue eyes ('the sign of a true Celt,' as she would incessantly remind her brown-eyed offspring) bleak as ice. When she was hostile, she would wax – this woman who herself used to remark that, at school, she had been taught nothing but which fork to use – quite abominably pompous.

She (pugnaciously, and apropos of absolutely nothing): I have done with human conversation. I have decided that, from now on, whatever anyone says to me, I shall simply categorise as either Fact or Opinion.

I: Fair enough. Well, I have to go to the library now.

She: *Aha*! Now, that is Fact.

I (foolishly): No, it's not. It's Opinion.

She: 'I have to go to the library.' That is a statement of pure fact.

I: No, it's only my opinion that I need to go.

She: My dear, good Gabrielle, may I remind you that the action of going to the library is one which . . .

Well, you get the picture.

When she was angry – which she too often was – she was vicious.

She was not, to be perfectly blunt, a conventionally good mother. She never quite stopped being that pampered youngest child who had charmed her way out of responsibility; never understood that, while bad things happen to us all, they must be mourned and moved on from; never grasped that situations might on occasion arise that did not intrinsically revolve around Mary. As she grew older, shielded from reality by a husband who never challenged her, and five children her procreation of whom absolved her from ever having seriously to listen to, so her selfishness and her volatility increased, her goodwill becoming more conditional, and her expectations of her own conduct dwindling to imperceptibility; towards the end of her life, she quite simply refused to have any dealings whatsoever with any single person – and no, that by no means excluded those to whom she had given birth – she found less than irresistibly enchanting. A year before she died, I complained to her, mildly, about a colleague. 'Ha!' she retorted, immediately and with feeling. 'You don't know you're born – you should have been in the WAAF!' It was then 1985: forty years since she had been required to make a sustained social effort of any kind.

In many ways, she did not have life easy. True, she was most happily married; and true, to a man who provided for her more than adequately in material terms: my mother never, ever, wondered where the next penny was coming from. But, on the other hand, she was born, poor woman, into a society whose professional expectation of her was that she spend her day cooking and cleaning – skills she did not possess, and, less conventional or more selfish than others of her kind, saw no reason in any great measure to acquire: she was far more interested in watching the news. She carried off her lack with considerable wit and style – and I must add, in fairness, that we none of us actually con-tracted bubonic plague – but I know it was difficult for her. More difficult still was that, as the century wore on, she began to see other women, some not too much younger than herself at all, who had very different visions of how their lives should be. Women who regarded a job outside the home not as a mark of poverty or self-indulgence, but as their inalienable right; women who found domestic ineffi-ciency a cause for faint amusement, not shame; women who were masters of their own time, who, unless they chose, need never bake another cake or fry another batch of chips again. She watched these women on television. She read about them in the newspaper. She raised one in her daughter.

I was her second child and only daughter, which latter was both a pleasure and a pain. On the one hand, she loved me with a very special love – a middle brother recently com-mented rather bitterly that she 'idolised' me – and, in that testosterone-rampant locker room that was my childhood home, she had reason to. I was female company, someone to talk hairstyles and diets with, someone to read her old Angela Brazil books, and later, her Keats and Shelley, and her beloved Rupert Brooke; someone more interested in defending Paul McCartney against Tyrone Power than Spurs against Arsenal. We were very good buddies, my mother and I. On Cup Final day, we used to leave sandwiches and crisps for the rest of the family, and go off to the pictures together; when I was older, we became fully fledged conspirators, drinking whiskey before lunch and singing Irish songs fer-vently off-key, secretly ogling Patrick McGoohan on *The*

Prisoner while everyone else was following the plot, making jokes about 'these bloody men', who comprised the rest of the family, and dissolving into guilty giggles when they would walk into the room.

She saw herself in me; on a good day, she admired me, on a bad day, she envied me. She saw the things I had that she lacked: the education, the independence, the career (as a journalist, no less, a professional gatherer of her all-important news), saw the single woman's existence that, viewed through her several pairs of deepest pink spectacles, appeared to revolve around my pleasure and mine alone. She saw, agonised over, in a shameful corner rejoiced in – and I do believe in many ways laid the foundation for – my consistently disastrous love life.

In the good Catholic circles in which we grew up, Herself was known (to what joy of her daughter may be imagined) as the woman with the four fine sons, and, oh, was she proud of them. She would declare, at childhood suppertimes, doling out burnt sausages and frozen crinkle-cut chips, that she wanted one son to be a doctor, and one to be a priest, and when, one afternoon, fired by *The Sound of Music* and my personal heroine, my third form teacher, Mother Mary Campion, I reassured her that the latter at least was covered, that I was going to be a nun, she was openly horrified. ('Oh, darling, *no*!') My brothers ate on, unmoved.

It was made crystal clear to me from the age of, oh, let's say thirteen, that my mother's handsome, witty, and loving husband, and her four fine sons, were her property and hers alone. Loyal and good and merry buddy as I was admitted, it was beyond negotiation that my role in the family movie was that of good chum to the sexy heroine, that, love me and laugh with me as my mother might, any noticeable femininity that was going around the Donnelly household was to be kept well away from the clutches of a thirty years younger interloper. Looking back now, in the calm achieved by years and distance, I can only shake my head in wonderment at some of the more baroque lengths she went to keep me neuter. There was the period around the time of my adolescence when my choices of knickers lay between my 50″ hipped grandmother's rejects, and Brendan's Y-fronts. There was the indecipherable water heating system, which mysteriously provided baths for my muddy small brothers but rarely for me, as a result of which Herself would accuse me, in tones of shocked outrage, of 'smelling dirty'. (When at last I discovered how to provide my own hot water – and, scarcely surprisingly, embarked upon a lifelong addiction to two baths a day – the charge slipped, effortlessly, to 'neurotic', and 'smelling of chemicals'.) There were the oh so hilarious jokes she would make about '*my* husband' and '*my* sons' – as opposed to my own neither – and the tenderly whimsical conversations she would have with the house's other female, the (spayed) dog, Sally: 'Yes, my darling, I know you'd *love* to have puppies, what a *shame* it is that you just don't have any sex appeal . . .' Can these things really have happened? My memory tells me quite firmly that they did, and I do not believe that I am delusional. I loved my mother. But it was not by accident that, in my twenties, I emigrated.

I went to Los Angeles: Europe was not big enough for the two of us. When, after a couple of years of travelling back and forth between the two places, I finally, and quite painfully, decided to make my home in a foreign country, I had to tell her on three separate occasions before she heard me. My father, defending her to the last, said that that was because the idea was too distressing for her to bear. It seemed to have occurred to no one that I might have liked someone to talk my decision over with. Which, of course, was one of the reasons why I left.

When I went, she was bereft. By then, she had cut herself off from most people outside the immediate family, and many within it; I had provided almost her only female company, and, when I left her alone with 'these bloody men', she was more sad – and far, far more angry – than I realised at the time. The anger revealed itself, over the years, and in strange and piecemeal ways. After her death, I learned that she had told a cousin – for no particular reason, and with not one shred of truth – that I was sharing an apartment with a gay couple ('and you can imagine what Pat thinks of *that*!'). I inherited the novel she had almost finished writing, a fictionalised account of the Barrett family, and discovered that it featured herself, her husband, and her four sons as herself, her husband, and her four sons, and me – and chillingly, it is quite unmistakably me – as someone else's daughter entirely, who asks her rather stupid mother for help in an unhappy love affair, fails to get it, and hangs herself. No, she was not happy with me; she was not, for a long time, happy with anything very much.

As the years passed, she came to accept my departure. The Irish in her, after all, was familiar with emigration; the Catholic approved America as home of the Kennedys and movies where Bing Crosby played a priest; the adventurer applauded, and the card-carrying flirt still remembered those large-boned, wry American airmen. Her own life, too, became brighter over the years. The messy small boys turned into men; she and my father moved from the gloomily functional barn where we children had grown up to a smaller house, cheerful and filled with light; they bought, and she decorated in an elegant, dramatic taste which had been starved through the years, a holiday flat in southern Spain.

The last time I visited England during her life, she told me she understood that I was living in the right place ('It's not as if you're going back home to an unhappy marriage'). It was a good visit, as all were not, necessarily; it was June, and we spent much time sitting in the garden in the sun. She told me – unblushingly, she who had ruled my father's life with a whim of iron for thirty-five years – that when he retired, she 'thought she could persuade Himself to move permanently to Spain'. She astonished me by interrupting an anecdote about an extremely minor moral decision with, 'Yes, you would do that: you're a *good* girl.' She added, darkly, 'Not like some.' She discovered, to her unutterable delight, that I knew all the lyrics to *Da-Doo-Ron-Ron*, and repeatedly forced me to sing it into an imaginary microphone, while my brother Kevin and she (the diagonal leg again) acted as my back-up dancers. The morning before I left we two spent strutting around the sitting room in a richly irreproducible comic fantasy involving, as far as I remember, Jeremy Irons and Princess Alexandra as eighteenth-century dandies (you had to be there), which made us both laugh so hard we had to keep stopping to clutch each other for support. Three months later, she was dead.

She died very suddenly. She had been troubled through August by a flu bug which would not go away; in September, she went into hospital for tests, was found to have viral pneumonia, and was prescribed penicillin shots; the same morning, she sent my father out to buy her a new tooth-brush holder, and told him that she would like to be moved from the public ward to a private room, but that he was to put the request in such a way as not to hurt the public ward nurses' feelings. Then she collapsed with a massive pulmonary embolism, and died within hours.

I received the news at 2.00 in the afternoon. By 6.00 that evening, I was on a night flight to London, my body sobbing uncontrollably, my mind as numb as an anaesthetised tooth. I went with her sister, my aunt Alicia, to see the body, and the sight of her lying, waxen, in her coffin, with her eyes closed, her rosary wound around her clasped hands, filled me with intense irritation. 'Oh, for heaven's sake!' I wanted to snap at the scenery-chewing old drama queen. 'Get up, and stop looking so *dead*!' Uncle Tony flew over from Rome to say the funeral Mass, after which we threw a suitably splendid party: we Catholics believe in giving our dead a good send-off.

The family house has changed since she has been dead. Once a comfortable home, it has become a place shared by my father and brother Kevin, two unmarried men. The framed photographs, the ornamental pots and knick-knacks that used to sit on surfaces have gone now, huddled forlornly into corners and cupboards, like guests ignored at a party. On the living room floor, half-finished crossword puzzles teeter on top of piles of Wisdens; the family supply of toilet paper (twelve in a pack for economy; acid green for reasons no one has adequately explained to me) stands proudly on display in the centre of the mahogany dining table. When I visit, once every year or so, I make a point of tidying up. I sort through months' old *Radio Times* and parish newsletters; I put shoes in bedrooms and broken radio pieces in the basement; I pick flowers from the tangled jungle that was once the garden. 'This looks nice,' my father and brother murmur, eyeing me with uneasy admiration, as if I had danced around a chicken bone and produced rain. At mealtimes, when I have insisted on conversation, they will linger for an extra glass of wine. 'There's nothing like a woman's touch,' my father will say. It is the closest we have come in our still difficult relationship: closer by far than I was allowed while Herself lived. Days after I have gone, the house will be exactly as it was.

They say, unanimously, and on every occasion, that I have my mother's face, although I cannot see it myself. What I do know, know bone deep, and will know till the hour of my death, is that she and I have inhabited the same body. It's a good body, of sturdy peasant stock, not elegant, but reasonably proportioned, with broad shoulders, big hands, and, happily, good legs; a touch heavier all over than is fashionable, but firm, and, most important of all, in excellent working order. So much for the flesh: but the identicalness runs deeper than that. It is there, ineradicable, in the carriage of the head, the instinctive positioning of the arms, in the relation of the shoulder to the thigh, the back of the skull to the fall of the eyelids. I never, ever wanted to wear my mother's clothes. But I actually quite like carrying around her body. It is, as I said, a good body: one of the better parts of her that, while I live, will never quite die.

I think I've turned out to be nicer that she was: I know I'm happier. I have had a good education, which she and my father provided for me, and her own lack of which must have caused a naturally intelligent woman frustrations I can only guess at. But then, I have also made a point of educating myself in skills that come no more naturally to me than they did to her. The skill, for instance, of listening to other people, instead of dismissing them when what they say becomes inconvenient; that of seeing others' good fortune as a cause for celebration, not envy; that of realising that happiness, if it exists, is a goal to be worked for, not a bar of chocolate handed down gratis when God is in a good mood. Maybe my mother, too, would have thought to acquire these skills had her mind been better trained. Maybe.

She has been dead for eight years now, and I have been emigrated for fourteen. For the first time in my life, so long has been her shadow, there is a man with whom I am discussing a profound commitment; for the first time, at this late stage of my childbearing years, I am thinking, if it is still possible, of having a child. What if we did have a child, and it were a daughter? I would teach her many things that my mother taught me. I would teach her strict morals, and an irreverence for temporal authority; I would encourage in her a sense of humour and a sense of spirituality; I would show her the joys of a good book, and insist that, however god-like seemed to her the object of her teenaged crush, he could never hold a candle to Paul McCartney. I would teach her *The Mountains of Mourne*, and *Hail, Glorious Saint Patrick*, and *The Snowy Breasted Pearl*. I would also hope to give her the things that I was not given: stability, and unconditional love, a relationship in which her needs were a little more important, not a little less, than mine; most important of all, I would make damned sure she knew and loved her father, and knew, too, that it was right for him to love her as well as me. I would do what I would lay bets it never occurred to my mother to do, and set out my aims, clearly, to that same father, and beg him to tell me if I strayed too far from them. I would pray that, unlike my mother, I could hear him if he did.

'Oh, yes!' snorts my mother's voice somewhere in the reaches of my soul. 'You and your clever theories of childraising – just wait till you've actually had one, chum.'

It's been a long wait, thank you, Mummy; it might even be eternal.

And yet, when she died, something went from my life that I know will never return. Our own particular brand of comradeship, our shorthand, our laughter. The love with which, on a good day, she would look at me; her occasional, exhilarating, kingfisher flashes of astonishing wisdom. Oh, yes, and whiskey before lunch.

We had a fight, one of our all too many, soon after I moved to Los Angeles, and I wrote her a furious letter, demanding to know when in our lives she and I could achieve 'some sort of normal, friendly relationship'. 'Probably never,' she wrote back, sadly and affectionately, in the spidery scrawl my own hand grows more and more to resemble. 'Because we are not normal friends, you and I. We are mother and daughter.'

I miss her.

William Granwick

'DON'T PUT YOUR DAUGHTER ON THE STAGE'

Yasmin Kureishi

When I was asked to write a piece on my relationship with my mother I couldn't help inwardly flinching. Now if I were to write something on my father, I know I would have felt much easier about the whole venture. Yes, I did have my ups and downs with my dad, especially in my teens when I started going out with boys, but the way we were together, and his effect on me, was so much more straightforward, more comfortable, than it has ever been with my mother.

Although my father, when he was alive, had a strong, positive influence on me, it was my mother who throughout my childhood and teenage years was the major influence in my life. With this in mind, it struck me first of all that I'd been sitting on a lot of stuff all these years that I had, for some reason, hardly dared to look at. This denial, this reluctance to probe too deeply into my psyche and examine the dynamics of our relationship and the repercussions on my life as it is now was, I felt, more than just 'taking the parental relationship for granted'. Rather, it told me about the underlying state of our relationship, the complexity of it all, the pain, the anger, the hurt, which is all mixed up with our deep love for one another, the humour that we share together, her generosity, the wonderful way she relates to my son and the fact she is broadminded enough to listen to my most intimate problems and offer advice rather than disapproval. All this creates a strong, emotional bond, a bond which is always there, intense, inescapable. And so this was now my opportunity to get off that seat, and unravel this most complicated of relationships.

I spent most of my childhood trying to please my mother. I sought her approval and always deferred to her wisdom and to some extent I think I still do. Ultimately, to earn her love and approval, I had to compensate for having a brother she found difficult to cope with. Hanif was the independent one; as soon as he could ride a bike he was off and there was nothing my mother could do about it. While my brother roamed the streets of Bromley on his bike, I stayed dutifully at home with Mum. I wore pretty dresses, played quietly and for the most part did what I was told.

However, my brief of playing the ideal daughter didn't stop there. I also had to fulfil the ambition she'd had herself as a young girl of becoming a ballet dancer. 'But you wanted to go to ballet lessons,' I hear her say. I can't say whether I wanted to or not. I didn't have wants as a child, they'd have been superfluous. I was an extension of her, not a person in my own right. All I knew was that going to ballet pleased her, and I got a great deal of attention from her because of it. There were the lessons to go to, ballet shoes to get, ribbons to sew on, ballet exams and auditions to pass. Why ballet? I ask myself. Why did she chose ballet, that most elusive of professions? Millions of girls aspire to its purity, its princess-like image, strive for the perfect body which is worshipped like some goddess. Hour upon hour of one's life is sacrificed to achieve that perfection. Yet so few actually make it, and that included me. I suppose it was unfortunate that physically I had all the right attributes necessary for a dancer. Mum wouldn't have had much success with an overweight tomboy! But it was inside my head that I wasn't really committed enough, though I would never have admitted it at the time. Also, I was painfully shy in those days and shunned the limelight; I preferred to be in the background somewhere, definitely not centre stage with the spotlight shining down on me.

Sacrifice bringing its own rewards is one of the central themes in Christianity. My mother was keen on sacrifice. Perhaps this Christian notion of sacrifice and martyrdom was passed down to her from her mother who was a regular churchgoer and Methodist Sunday school teacher. But all I knew then was that she'd sacrificed her life for her family, and that she'd said often enough that she didn't want me to end up like her, with hands permanently in the kitchen sink. Yet by her wanting me to be a ballet dancer, and not allowing me to find my own way, she didn't seem to realise that she was sacrificing my individuality to her needs.

My father was the sole financial provider and my mother, like millions of other mothers of that generation and before, became the one who provided for all our other basic needs. When I think back I can see that it was my father who was the dominant presence in our household, who constantly made his likes and dislikes known to all, whereas it was apparent that my mother didn't expect to be – and so wasn't – treated as a person in her own right. The knock-on effect has been that she has never validated my needs. I felt this most acutely when my son Edward was born and she assumed that I would be following that same sacrificial path. 'I never left you,' she'd say when I yearned for an evening out or, 'You can't expect to have time to write when you have child to look after.' I did walk her way for a while, when Edward was a baby. And what hard years they were! I was a wreck. I didn't care what I ate, what I looked like, what clothes I wore, what I watched on television. In other words, I'd become like she had been when we were children. I'd mirrored her behaviour, but I didn't stop there. I took several steps more than my mother along that sacrificial path by putting up with my then husband's verbal and emotional abuse. He didn't validate my needs either, my rights or my dignity as a human being. He loathed me having my own opinions, feelings or life if they in an way differed from his own. What is even more horrifying to me now is that I put up with this oppressive way of living without any kind of realisation of what was happening. It was as if I'd slipped back into childhood with my mother imposing her will on me and me just accepting it, wanting to please. But then I don't think I ever really thought about myself or what I wanted, until I realised how extreme his behaviour was, and that for my own sanity I could not endure this way of living indefinitely.

As a child, I saw my mother as always tired and harassed. I felt for her and frequently took her side when she and Dad argued. I yearned to make her life happier. But looking at her life then, I can see that she couldn't find fulfilment in her own life because she lacked the confidence, the motivation, the know-how. These are the qualities that my father had. It wasn't that my father was endowed with more intelligence than my mother; it was, rather, a difference in attitude. She hadn't seen people achieving in her life. My father, on the other hand, had watched his father, brothers and sisters achieving success in all areas. His father was a colonel and a doctor in the Indian army, his brothers went to Harvard and Cambridge and then became high flyers in their fields of work. My mother could have built up her confidence over the years but she was stifled by my father's uneasiness about his wife becoming as educated or as cultured as himself. This only served to reinforce her feelings of self-worthlessness and so my mother took it upon herself to be the nurturer of 'greatness' rather than the 'greatness' itself. Like a lot of men, both my father and my brother disliked ballet; it didn't have enough intellectual meat on it for their liking. Cricket, literature and music was their diet. So ballet became my mother's exclusive domain. It was something she loved, that she could have as her own, where she could see herself achieving something, albeit through me, which was apart from them, which would give her some value.

Yet my mother had not been without talent, opportunities or beauty. Unfortunately for her, though, her parents were from a stratum of society that knows its place and finds aspirations, especially of the artistic kind, uncomfortable. It wasn't all right to be an artist if you were lower middle class. You could be a shopkeeper like her father or a secretary, yes, but not an artist. My mother passed the entrance exam to a commercial college where she could learn shorthand and typing. She'd also passed the art school entrance exam. Her parents wanted her to go to the former, she wanted to go to the latter and that was where she had landed up, at art school. Her reason for going to art school was simply because her best friend was going. On similar lines, I passed the audition to go to ballet school and I chose to go there partly to please my mum and partly to escape racism at our local primary school. I think it is quite revealing that, in our younger years, Mum and I used such puny reasoning to make important life-changing decisions. I'm sure we're not the only women to have done this. Could it be that as women we don't really take ourselves and our careers seriously enough?

My mother thoroughly enjoyed going to art school, the freedom of it all, being a student, having boyfriends, visiting the great antiquities of Italy and Spain. It opened up a different world for her, a world of culture, a world that a young woman from her class rarely experienced. Normally a girl from her background would have left school at fourteen and got a job in a shop or an office if they were lucky, then waited for a man to come along and rescue them. My mum didn't leave art school until she was twenty-one. But she took her art no further. Once again there are parallels between us both. Like me with my ballet dancing, she didn't follow it through and make a career out of her art training. We gave up when it came to the gutsy part of trying to find a starting point to launch our careers. We collapsed when faced with the competitive fierceness of the art world, the challenge of making it. We were too scared, too unconfident. Moreover, we both expected it all to be handed to us on a plate. I expected to get into the Royal Ballet straight away, even though I'd never seen a brown swan before! My mother wanted to be like Picasso. We never dreamt of taking second best. My mother could have become a lecturer in art like her best friend went on to become, or in my case, I could have become a ballet teacher, but we chose not to. Due to my father's constant pressure I did go to college and took my O and A levels, then I went on and got a degree. My mother ended up working in a bank until she got married and had kids.

She found being a housewife tedious and soul destroying. She was certainly no earth mother, baking cakes, making curtains, growing vegetables. Even gossiping with the other mums in the playground when she came to pick us up was disagreeable to her. But then, this had never been the role model she'd had as a child. My mother's own mother had from an early age been hardened by the ways of the world. My grandmother's mother, a deeply religious woman who didn't let her two daughters sew or knit on the sabbath, had been an invalid for many years. My grandmother to this day can't understand why her mum married someone like her father who was a great drinker and spent all his spare time down the pub. She recalls her mother saying that she often wondered when they were courting why he always took her back home at ten o'clock in the evening. After she married him she found out the truth: that it was to get in some drinking time before the pub shut. My grandmother, now ninety-four, vividly remembers that at the age of fourteen, when her mother died, she'd had to drag her drunken father out of the pub as his wife's hearse was slowly making its way to the cemetery.

At the age of fourteen, when my great-grandmother died, my grandma left school and started working for the Post Office, and there she remained until she retired at the age of seventy-six. She was, and still is, a strong, independent-minded woman. I remember asking her once whether she'd been in the suffragette movement and getting quite excited at the vision of her fighting for women's right to vote. I forgot that someone from her background, in those days, especially in her situation, wouldn't have had the time to contemplate the unfairness of women's position in society, or to go on marches or be chained to railings. They just had to get on with living, surviving. She'd looked pretty horrified when I asked her, as if I'd insulted her. So my mum, as a child, had before her this odd mixture of strength, coupled with an underlying belief in the inferiority of women.

My grandmother's husband didn't support her or my mother. He kept all his money for himself, for fags and beer. Consequently, my grandmother didn't give up work when she married my grandfather, like other women would have done at that time, nor did she when she had my mother. My grandfather also frequently verbally abused his wife. My mother loathed him because of the way he treated her mother; she had little time or respect for him. Yet, funnily enough, I always got on well with my grandfather. Grandma and Grandad lived in our house for several years while we were young. I often sought out Grandad's company. He fascinated me, largely I think because he was so different from my father. But I always sensed he was not the person to go to if you were in trouble. He died when I was eighteen. I married someone who had quite a lot in common with him. Particular types of relationships, like behaviour, can be handed down from generation to generation, their patterns perpetuated, influenced or modified by situations or events.

The amount of hard work, effort and money my mother put into fulfilling her ambitions for me was amazing. 'Don't put your daughter on the stage' never came into it. She went out to work full-time to pay for my ballet school fees. She took me up to London to the Royal Academy of Dancing every Saturday and somehow or other fitted in the washing and shopping as well. This dedication and sacrifice (as I saw it then) by my mother made me feel even more sorry for her and made me determined that I couldn't fail her. My father was against this whole ballet thing right from the start. He said I wasn't cut out to be a ballet dancer, I was too introverted. He wanted me to be a writer. The family felt split in my early teens, with Dad pushing my brother in one direction and Mum pushing me in another. But whereas my brother only had to listen to one voice, I was hearing conflicting views on what I should do with my life. In the end I gave up dancing and Dad took me over. Mum immediately took a more secondary role in my life. She gave in gracefully, accepting that Dad, after all, was right. But how did Mum feel about me not making it as a ballet dancer? My mother says now that she was upset, and she sometimes thought about all that wasted time and money, but if I didn't have the dedication there wasn't much point in her pushing me. She said that she thought I had the talent to make it as a ballet dancer – but then she was just like all those other mums at the Royal Academy thinking their darling daughter was the best.

My cultural identity was another area where my mother's controlling influence took a firm hold. She did this by discouraging any kind of recognition of the part of me that was Indian. My father, who was quite Anglicised anyway, having gone to an English public school in India, probably thought this was the best approach, considering that we were born in England and growing up here. Dad came to England from India in his early twenties to study aeronautical engineering at London University. This was an ill-suited choice made by his authoritarian father. After all, here was someone who had difficulties putting a light bulb in a socket or mending a fuse. He soon gave up the course and switched to economics which he found extremely dry. His father refused to give him any more money, and he ended up getting a job in the Pakistan Embassy where he remained until he retired. In his spare time, when he wasn't browsing around in second-hand bookshops, my father wrote some very good articles for various magazines. But his true love was fiction, and eventually he gave up writing articles so that he could write novels. Sadly, he never made it in this field, although he proved to be a great source of inspiration and encouragement to both my brother and myself.

It was while Dad was working at the Pakistan Embassy that

he met my mother. They fell madly in love. Race, class or religion didn't come into it. However, Dad's family weren't at all pleased about him marrying an English woman. And only two of Dad's brothers out of twelve children came to the wedding. I never met his mother and can only vaguely remember his father. Dad had a brother and a sister who had settled in England whom we used to see quite a lot. We also frequently saw some of his brothers and their families when they came over from Pakistan. Because they had disapproved of the marriage, my mother was quite critical of them and she didn't particularly encourage us to be friendly with them. This might have had the effect of isolating me from my cultural roots but I can hardly blame my mother for it. She must have felt rejected and isolated from their world because of their initial reaction to her.

Although my father adhered to the Muslim rule of not eating pork, he was in some important ways a liberated man for his generation and background. He did his share of the work around the house. He wasn't any good at DIY, but he did make various attempts in this direction. He often cooked curries and every weekend he hoovered and dusted the whole house. He also entrusted my mother with the cheque book and all household financial matters. As I've said, like a lot of men of all races and backgrounds, he held my mother back intellectually and socially, but his approach towards me was entirely different. He wanted me to be educated, to have a profession, to be financially independent and to see myself in no way inferior to any man. He also wanted to see me happily married to a man of my choice. I did feel this pressure to be married and have children as I got into my late twenties. It was partly because of this that I made the hasty decision to marry. My mother, on the other hand, interestingly enough, never encouraged me to get married. In fact she always said, 'Don't get married'. Although in many ways she was happily married to my father, I think she found playing the subservient role in her marriage hard work and unsatisfying, particularly as she was someone who was not naturally inclined towards such a passive existence.

Whilst my father's family were against his marriage, my mother's parents wholeheartedly approved of the match. They adored their son-in-law and lived in his house harmoniously until, with two growing children, it became too cramped. Coming from a big family in India, my father was used to an extended family and so living together felt quite natural to him. My mother tells me no one was outwardly critical of her marriage, which seems strange considering we lived in a suburban area where a brown or black face in the fifties and sixties was a rarity. But she says now she feels we have suffered because of our mixed cultural identity. Yes, we did suffer, though I take a more positive view. I see my dual parentage as an enrichment of my life. My mother dealt with our mixed cultural identity the only way she knew how. Any emotional feelings, anything too uncomfortable, were swept under that all too English carpet. As a child, if I happened to mention something about me being different from the other kids in school, my mother would say, 'You're English, you were born here,' and that was the end of the story. In fact, I never told my mother that I was experiencing racism at school. I felt ashamed. It was such a strict unspoken rule that I didn't know until I was in my mid teens that my brother had also suffered at school. I'd taken it all personally, blaming myself for being such a disgusting person it could only happen to me. If either of us had known what the other was experiencing we could have been some support to each other but instead we were isolated from each other.

As I got into my twenties, I yearned more and more to know about that other part of me. My father, seeing how much I needed to seek out my roots, paid for me to go to

Pakistan, where his family had settled after partition. This did me the world of good. I returned oozing self-confidence and understanding much more about myself and my father's background. I had felt really at home there. I felt I belonged there. Dad wrote in his journal when I returned from my trip, 'Quite honestly Pakistan is the right place for her. She will suddenly flower out. I know that much.' And, 'She should go there in her own right and not dependent on people.' But I never did go there to live.

In her early sixties my mother changed, grew tougher and more assertive. She kicked away altruism and started to give herself some nourishment. I could see this happening even before Dad died. She began to do more things which she enjoyed, and she still does. She goes to art exhibitions, films, theatre, goes away with friends. She even went away for a weekend on her own. She leads a full life. You name it, my mother does it. I admire the way she's become her own person. For years she was there for me alone. Sometimes I still view her as the old Mum and find it difficult to accept this new life. She says you have to make an effort when you're on your own. It's either that or sink, and my mother is too spirited to do the latter. But we are close by to support each other when necessary. We live a mile apart, and my grandmother is just up the road from my mother. We're quite a devoted trio really. My mother rings me up every day and she goes to see her mother several times a week. When Dad died, Mum and I poured out our misery to each other, talked about him endlessly and cried a lot. We understood each other's pain better than anyone else could.

In some ways I feel I am only just discovering the real me, where I am, where I want to be. What do I want from life? Do I really want this? Can I say no? These are the questions that at the age of thirty-five I have just begun to ask myself. And because I am only now asserting my own needs and wants, my relationship with my mother has become more stormy. I will no longer comply with her point of view just to please her and she finds this hard to accept. All I can say is that my relationship with my mother is an extremely complex business, but by sifting through our past, I can now see more clearly where my mother and I are coming from. I certainly view my mother with a little more understanding.

GOODBYE TOMORROW

Jeanine McMullen

They play *As Time Goes By* quite a lot on the radio these days and people think of Humphrey Bogart and Ingrid Bergman smouldering with unspent passion on the brink of war. But I resent that. That's my mother's song and she's not singing it in a gin palace in Casablanca. She's pounding it out on an old joanna, both of them relentlessly out of tune, in the dim and dusty private parlour of a rickety pub somewhere in the mid-west of New South Wales. Outside the air is dead with heat, the locusts are strumming monotonously and from the public bar comes the massed roar of the Australian male trying to get drunk before closing time. The smell of stale beer, dusty roads and the outside dunny fight with the waft of expensive perfume my mother had splashed on with the same gallant recklessness she's attacking the piano, singing 'With a tear in my voice, just like Vera Lynn' and smiling at me, her audience of one, not knowing that every word of that song hurts like hell. I was deeply suspicious of all that sighing and kissing and people needing their mates, which she took care to emphasise.

My mother was a great one for using the words of songs to make a point. I wished on stars, took every April raindrop as a falling violet, dreamt of white Christmases, understood, if somewhat forlornly, that we'd meet again, someway, somewhere, as I was packed off to boarding school; knew that jealousy would be my undoing, always let my conscience be my guide, acknowledged that into each life some rain must fall, that you couldn't trust the whispering grass, believed that over the rainbow was really the best place to be and, above all, that no matter how bad things were, tomorrow was another day. Dennis Potter may have used songs as the background to the dramas of everyday life; my mother used everyday life as the background for the songs. But *As Time Goes By* was different. Perhaps she sang it more often and probably I sensed (or thought I did) a genuine longing in her voice, because, when I was nine years old, the chance of her finding a permanent man was, apart from us losing her handbag, the most frightening thing I could think of.

The handbag was a very large, squashy one. It had to be because inside it was everything that linked us to the past and made our present life possible; my mother's nursing certificates and badges, her authorisation as a JP, my grandmother's ring and the watch she'd bought for me just before she died which was to be given to me when I was twenty-one, photographs, a vast litter of combs and pills and lotions we might need and, most importantly, the money to pay our bills. As we wandered from place to place, when I wasn't worried about my mother getting lost, I was guarding the handbag.

My father had been discarded not long after I was born and he was only around then because my conception had been the result of a trial reconciliation; one of many that led nowhere except into more of the hell their marriage had been made in. My mother should never have been married to anybody and my father needed an amiable doormat, not the free spirit he tried to mould into one.

Like so many Australian men at the time, his mates came first and frustration at my mother's independence made him spiteful. When I say he was around when I was born, he was actually locked in the bathroom where my grandfather had dumped him to stop him going off to play in a tennis match. As soon as he was released and knew he had a daughter, he sneaked off and registered me as 'Jeanine' when my mother had desperately wanted to call me something else. That was the final, unforgivable crime, so out went my father and for me to use 'that tart's name', let alone his surname, was like spitting on the bible. Even when I grew older and had to sign official documents with my registered name, I felt as if my fingers would drop off. Everyone in my mother's large family warned me early on that to have anything to do with my father was to be the worst kind of traitor, but happily used him as a threat if I misbehaved. I wasn't afraid of him physically, but on the rare occasions when he was allowed to take me out for the day, he not only called me by the forbidden name, but seemed incredibly boring. My mother on the other hand was wild, funny, glamorous, full of magic and dreams and surprises and carelessly happy to pack me into her luggage, along with any spare bits of livestock we had on hand, and go where we fancied.

For the first few years of my life she had been able to leave me with my grandmother, Nan, while she went out to earn our living, usually as a nurse, but she'd take on anything that interested her, even politics for a while which is how she was made a JP. I don't think I realised she was my mother in those days. There were so many of the family living at home, gay young aunts and uncles revolving around the small contented world I inhabited with Nan, so that my mother was just another one of the courtiers who brought toys and clothes and treated me like a doll.

When Nan became terminally ill, the butterfly days were over and we began those journeys which never really ended. Then it was to find a cure for Nan. We trailed from climate to climate: the mountains, the dry interior, back to the sea air again, and it was all made to seem the most enormous adventure and that this time the miracle of Nan getting better would happen as soon as we arrived. To distract me, when it didn't, there were the surprises: it might be a puppy pulled out of someone's pocket, a Prince Charming all dressed up in panto gear come to take us for a drive in a carriage drawn by a white pony, and there were the stories and the songs, always the songs.

When Nan finally died in spite of all her efforts, my mother's grief was so terrible that she collapsed and landed up in hospital herself. The aunts, most of whom were now married (unhappily on the whole) saw to it that I realised that if anything happened to my mother I'd either be sent to live with my father or have to go to an orphanage. To them it was just casual conversation; to me, at five years old, it was a nightmare. It was then that my obsession with my mother began.

I had adored Nan who had been a strong haven in the fluctuating life around us. Now, it seemed to me, my mother was the one who needed protecting. Apart from the hospital which might take her off and kill her, there were the various men who inevitably tried to invade our lives (and I didn't want to be stuck with another father), and there were the aunts who constantly put my mother down but were very happy to raid our precious handbag. Already, to me, that bag had become a symbol of our security, but my mother had an overdeveloped sense of loyalty to her family and was absurdly generous to anyone needing a handout. I was enough of my father's daughter to see only disaster ahead.

At first after Nan died and my mother emerged from hospital, life was fairly stable. That was the era of the shops. The general idea was that by taking on the lease of some small retail outlet, my mother would acquire both accommodation and a business and be on hand to look after me. It didn't seem to matter what kind of business, all suggestions were accepted, like Pop's that she should open a fruit and veg shop. My grandfather, a big wild man who adored animals and was my constant ally against authority, had an old one-eyed racehorse he'd rescued and the fruit and veg shop had a shed in the yard big enough to house him. So Ginger and his cart and Pop went on the staff and picked up the produce from Paddy's Market every morning. When I didn't have to go to school I went with them, which is how Dolores the goat, Magnolia the duck and endless cats and dogs joined us, all of them pitied and purchased from the market and brought home on Ginger's cart, to be fed and tolerated by my mother. The shop did well as my mother had a great talent for selling things, but eventually the relations began to drift in and eat the profits, so she cheerfully removed the lot of us to another distant suburb where Dolores and Magnolia caused chaos, the relations picked up our trail and descended in even more voracious hordes, and there was nothing to do but begin our journeys again.

In between the trains and the boats and the country pubs, there were bush hospitals and remote sheep stations, lots of schools where I made brief and lonely appearances, even a few appallingly anxious periods at boarding schools where I lived in terror of what my mother was up to without my guiding hand to keep her from ruining us. Back in Sydney, if we didn't have yet another shop, we stayed with Aunty Ann who was married to an SP bookmaker. And that was a new terror, always waiting for the police to raid (although they never did because Uncle Happy paid them off), or for Uncle Happy to come home and find the sisters smoking or Aunty Ann gambling (both forbidden to his own family) and having to whisper in case we woke him up.

One night, after a dreadful quarrel with Aunty Ann, we ended up on a deserted Bondi Beach, completely homeless and quite exhausted. We'd been trailing around looking for a room all day, but with Sydney full of American troops, accommodation was impossible, especially if you had a child in tow. So we sat on the beach gazing at the stars while the surf whispered at our feet, my mother gaily singing *Tomorrow is Another Day* as I clutched the handbag and worried. But as usual my mother was right and along came a kindly police-man who rescued us and put the strong arm on one of the Bondi landladies till she gave us her best room for as long as we needed it. There was something about my mother which always caused someone to come to our aid with no strings attached.

I'd have sat on Bondi Beach for the rest of my life rather than go to boarding school or live with my father, but that night must have worried her because not so long after I was packed off again while she attempted the final reconciliation in order to give us a permanent home. Like so many of my mother's impulses, it was not well thought out. She and my father stayed together just long enough to conceive my brother and this time she was so anxious to get away from him that I was plucked from boarding school and back we went to the endless travelling, taking private nursing jobs, working as a receptionist in country hotels, anything with accommodation and a long way from Sydney.

Actually, my mother liked living in hotels. She was a true gypsy at heart and loved moving on when she felt like it. Possessions bothered her. Her handbag ('We can always buy what we need when we get there'), a bed and someone else to cook the meals, and she could get on with life. I was the one who insisted on a suitcase, dragging it along till she took it from me impatiently. But if life on the road had its problems, it was better than living in Sydney. There my mother was treated like a poor relation. She was just 'good old Rene', ready to give her last penny and fill in the gap. Everywhere else we went she was a star, belonging to the glitter and the spangles and, no matter how basic our surroundings, when she came into a room, all the circus came too.

This time of course, she was carrying my brother, but it didn't seem to make much difference, although we did tend to stop longer in any one place than before. She had promised me a brother but I thought she'd just produce him out of the handbag like all the other surprises, which for all the fuss she made about it could well have been true.

In fact she put both their lives at risk by refusing to go into hospital and leave me, practically swallowing a sheet as she muffled her screams in case I heard. I was too busy giving cheek to the midwife who treated me like a child and kept me out of the way so that I couldn't keep an eye on my mother or the handbag.

After my brother was born we went back to Sydney and Aunty Ann, who was once more in crisis. Eventually I was sent to boarding school again, never knowing where I'd be for the holidays . . . there were more shops, a bush nursing centre 120 miles west of Bourke, Aunty Ann's place. I just took the train ticket from the nuns at the last minute and waited for someone to meet me at the other end. Once I was sent to stay with some rather grand relations of one of the nuns, because my mother was off being married to a man years younger than herself and they and my brother were roaming around New South Wales in his 1928 Chevrolet with a sheepdog, a canary and a guitar and having the time of their lives. It was a very long time before I forgave any of them except the sheepdog and the canary.

I joined them at innumerable locations for the holidays and wove around myself a world of books and music and a lot of funny ideas I'd picked up from the nun's relations. My mother changed too. When she and my stepfather finally settled in a small country town, seeing that I was turning out to be a very strange girl, she decided to give my brother a more sane and ordinary background. She broadened her accent, joined the local Country Women's Association (and corrupted them into playing endless poker games), took up cooking and some minimal housework, made cakes for the various church bazaars (all denominations) and played 'Housie' (or Bingo) relentlessly. In fact, she melted into the crowd, except where I was concerned. Money was found to send me to a better convent in Sydney, more money to send me abroad with a French family and even more to find me and haul me home when I ran away from them. And much later, when I became a teacher in Sydney, she was there in the country to give homes to the stray cats, a duck with a clutch of ducklings and any other livestock the children brought to me for safekeeping; even once the plants from an entire garden which I'd dug up to save them from being buried under builder's rubble. All of them, animals and plants, were sent back on the night train to Cooma, collected at the other end and became part of the family.

Eventually, when I came home to stay and teach, I had the only decent room in the tiny house. My mother tolerated my friends patronising her, fed them and me royally, encouraged all the madness of that time when I worked and played very hard, dreamt impossible dreams, littered the place with rejected lovers for her to console, and took her completely for granted. Underneath the surface of our different lives, however, there was a strange psychic understanding. It was as if we were still on the road, living in our own particular world of memories and jokes, casually drifting in and out of each other's minds. It was commonplace for one of us to come into a room and continue in mid-sentence a conversation we'd been having quite silently, each of us in different parts of the house or garden. Less contentedly we shared the same aches and pains. Once I was taken to hospital with an injured back and woke from a drugged sleep to find my mother in the next bed, having been stricken in the night with the same symptoms.

I wonder now if all the fears and loneliness I'd felt so deeply as a child hadn't been picked up from her. Was all that singing and the magic and the surprises her way of masking her own terrors from me? Certainly the spoiling was to make up for the lack of a proper home, the banishments to boarding school ('At least I knew you'd have a roof over your head and three square meals a day' – ever the optimist, my mother) and the whispering terrors of life with Uncle Happy. But in one respect she was utterly ruthless. She always encouraged me to go after what I wanted, no matter how improbable it was, but I had to go after it alone.

When I was about nine years old, wanting to make our fortune, I decided to be a child star. I'd heard about an audition for a film. My mother was quite happy for me to apply, but I was on my own. She and Aunty Ann gave me my tram fare and sent me off with their blessing. I was the only child there alone, being pushed and sneered at by a mob of hysterical mothers, primping and prodding their kids and simpering at the producer. I didn't stand a chance, but when I arrived home limp and disillusioned, my mother and aunt dolled themselves up in their war paint and stormed along to see the producer himself. I was left behind in agony, while they pushed past the assistants, raged into the great man's office and wiped the floor with him. When, grovelling, he begged to see 'your dear little girl' again, they told him what he could do with his miserable film and, on the way out, demanded of the triumphant mothers what they thought they were doing putting their children in a dirty film. Didn't they know it was a dirty one? Oh well . . . And left the mothers storming into the producer's office to finish him off.

I learnt a lot from that. I not only had to go after what I wanted alone; if I failed I shut up about it. So alone I enrolled myself in schools, courses, jobs and later many things for which I had no real qualifications except my persistence in demanding to see the top person. ('Never bother with the help,' my mother always told me. 'Go to the top. The others are a waste of time.' It was when I forgot her advice that things began to go wrong.) But if she wasn't prepared to go with me on my quests, when I succeeded no one applauded louder than my mother or did so much to make sure the path ahead was as smooth as she could make it. That was what she dedicated herself to doing for the last years of our lives together.

I had never been able to tolerate the Australian heat, so when I finally made my way back to Europe and found that the asthma and chronic hayfever I'd suffered from disappeared, I stayed. The link with my mother was just as strong in spite of the twelve thousand miles between us. The phone would ring if I was ill or on the edge of despair, my mother at the other end declaring that she hadn't been able to sleep or had suffered a terrible phantom pain and was I all right? Parcels arrived with something I urgently needed or a notice from the bank to say money had been deposited just as the rent was due. A few times she appeared in person, once with my brother in tow, but when he finally married and settled, she came and stayed for the next fourteen years.

It was then that our relationship reversed itself. I was the provider, the instigator of impossible schemes, the one who gave the magic surprises, the one who left and she the one who stayed at home. People were surprised that I could live with my mother, at first in a tiny flat in London and later in a cold, remote farmhouse in Wales. There had been plenty of men ('A bloody League of Nations,' said my mother), but my childhood had given me a pathetically low boredom threshold. I was bitterly opposed to getting married and my mother was the only person I ever knew who kept the party going in all times and weathers. And I didn't need her to remind me that men may come and men may go, but mothers stick with you for ever and they don't really change.

Even Arthur, my stepfather, who'd begun their life together as willing to go anywhere and do anything as she was, had become sedate and settled; my own current man who'd been full of wild schemes and eccentricities had begun to sound very depressing about the future. With him finally gone to mix with the grown-ups, my mother and I sank into our mutual fantasy world with satisfaction.

Her years of enforced domesticity had turned my mother into a brilliant cook but one who always needed loud and frequent applause, which I was delighted to give her, having known her when even a boiled egg had been difficult. So she fed me and my growing horde of animals and our visitors with style and dash; she revelled in my tiny spark of fame on the radio and adored seeing off importunate fans, to my horror. During the years when neither fame nor fans nor money came to our door, she supported me when I wilted, and was there to keep my feet on the ground when the good times came back. Our loyalty to each other was total. Outsiders, appalled at the way we sometimes yelled at each other, sympathised with one or the other and were met with frozen silence and the knowledge that they would never be welcome again.

To other people my mother may have looked like an elderly, grey-haired, rather stout lady in unsuitable clothes for her age. She toddled around in outsize jeans and layers of ill-assorted cardigans at home and in bright red dresses (which I'd bought for her) when going out. But I saw her quite differently. To me she was still the elegant, brightly dressed, laughing creature with the tumble of auburn hair cascading over her shoulders who met me at the station when I came home from boarding school, making all the hatted and gloved mothers click their tongues but eye her secretly with envy. Within minutes she'd be chatting to them as if she'd known them for ever, making them all girls together and, if they hadn't had their disapproving offspring on hand, would probably have whisked them off to the nearest party. I could never get used to people calling her old.

My mother was a mix of cynic and romantic; prude and flirt; street arab and duchess. She was witty and wicked, horrendously untidy and brave as a terrier. None of those qualities deserted her in age. Like so many ex-nurses, she was a bit of a hypochondriac at times, but silently stoic when she was really ill. She contracted shingles and must have been in terrible pain but, knowing I had a deadline to meet, didn't give me a clue until she knew I was free to help her.

We were very different people. She could say outrageous things and make a friend for life; I can smile and make an enemy. I was always reaching higher than my station; it never occurred to her that she had a station. She was quick where I'm a bit on the slow side really; she could handle figures and money wonderfully, whereas I am hopeless with both. She never gave a damn what people thought of her and could not understand my horror of disapproval. I liked my books literary and my music serious; a 'nice polite murder' and Vera Lynn in full tearful voice were good enough for her. As the years went by, we met on the middle ground of books and music and, if she was the gardener and I was more interested in the animals, we helped each other out with plant and beast as the need arose.

Two things we shared fully: our sense of the ridiculous and our interest in the occult. We read the cards, the cups, the stars, the portents and the omens, believing them if it suited us and sneering when it didn't. That each of us would survive death was absolutely certain.

'So don't worry when I go,' my mother said many times. 'You won't get rid of me that easily. And I'll make sure no one upsets you. Do a bit of steady haunting. I'll enjoy that!'

And I believed her. That she would die was the greatest terror of all. Against that one appalling thought, nothing mattered. And yet always, I felt that she wouldn't somehow. She couldn't, not after all we'd been through. But of course she did, back home in Australia when the Welsh winters defeated not her spirit but her body. In the heat, she survived for another seven years, with her own little flat at last and my brother and his family to look after her far more sensibly and better than I ever had. But still the mind-link was there. Until the end, when her main concern was that I was not to be worried. I did know she was very ill, but as usual I dithered and dallied until it was too late, sure that she'd wait for me as she always had.

Since then, nothing. No mind-link, no sense of her presence, no light, no laughter. As for the supernatural and life after death and all that, they can keep it. I don't even bother to wish on a star any more. There doesn't seem much point now that the circus has gone for good. I just wish they wouldn't play *As Time Goes By* quite so much.

DAUGHTERS OF A HIDDEN CHILD

Hester and Marianne Velmans

Marianne: When I was asked to write a piece about my mother, the first thought that came into my head was that I couldn't do it.

Hester: Oh? Why not?

Marianne: I mean I can't talk about '*my* mother'. I can't talk about '*my* father', '*my* school', either. The singular pronoun implies disloyalty. Hypocrisy, even. There's something about being a twin . . .

Hester: I'd have the same problem.

Marianne: It's not *my* mother, it's *our* mother. And then I get this little voice whispering in my ear – '*freak*'. Being different from the other children. Remember?

Hester: I know. It's not just that you can't help using the royal 'we'; it's also that when you recall an event from the

201

past, you often can't remember which one of us actually experienced it.

Marianne: You've got to admit it's ironic – all those years of struggling to establish our individual identities, and it's still impossible to separate out the strands of that joint childhood of ours. I can't even lay claim to my relationship with my mother – *our* mother – without including you.

Hester: She was the ideal mother, you've got to give her that. When we needed her, as very young children.

Marianne: The centre of the universe.

Hester: No *I* was the centre of the universe. And you belonged there too. I'd say she was peripheral, but crucial. She was Atlas, she carried our world in her arms.

Marianne: You're right, I suppose she was peripheral. We didn't need anyone else – being an identical twin comes with a built-in guarantee that there is one person in the world who will always understand you. How can anyone, even a mother, compete with that?

Hester: She has always been sensitive to that. She never tried to compete or come between us. She was so careful not to play favourites. We were never jealous of each other, because she made certain there was never a sense of competition. We could always be sure of having the exact same measure of her love.

Marianne: But later on, we became aware of the way other people tried to play us off against each other. Do you remember how many times we were asked which one of us was better at maths, which one was better at English?

Hester: And then they'd proceed to tell us which one was prettier, which one was nicer . . .

Marianne: It's a wonder we didn't kill each other.

Hester: Right! But Mam would have none of it. She stuck to the story that neither of us was better or worse than the other in any way. She didn't pretend that we were exactly the same – I suppose she knew it was important to acknowledge the differences – but she would not allow any value judgements.

Marianne: Well, this may sound like a value judgement on my part, but I honestly thought she was better than other mothers. She used to throw amazingly inventive birthday parties for us, didn't she? She sat and made things with us.

Hester: I'm sure that's why I still have this obsessive need to make things for people instead of simply buying presents. She told us that things we made with our own hands came from the heart.

Marianne: I do so little of that with my children. She had a lot of time for us. She was always there for us.

Hester: But remember what it was like later, when we were in secondary school and she resumed her postgraduate studies – didn't we feel abandoned then?

Marianne: A little. We couldn't stand her having other interests, not being there for us all the time. She'd spoiled us: we had never counted on her wanting a life of her own. But my children have had to put up with a tired, distracted mother from the very start. I'm always out at the office, and when I *am* home I've usually got my nose in a manuscript or a pile of papers.

Hester: I know you feel guilty about that, but who's to say that isn't the best thing for them? I mean, here I am – I quit my job to have kids, and yet I have as many doubts as you. The idea that you can dedicate yourself to being a full-time mother for a finite period, and then get on with your own life, is fundamentally flawed. Your children won't really understand, no matter how old they are. I see that now that I am trying to clear more time for my writing.

Marianne: Still, Mam remained the central presence in our

life. Even after she started studying again. Much greater, at any rate, than Daddy. She controlled us; he indulged us.

Hester: And we tolerated him. He was the odd man out in a house of women.

Marianne: Oh, I don't know . . .

Hester: Yes! He'd stride out of the room if the conversation got too intimate. Talking about your period in front of him was totally taboo.

Marianne: He was away such a lot, on business trips.

Hester: Even if he hadn't been, it would have been the same thing. He just wasn't part of the club. She was.

Marianne: She turned to him for help in disciplining us.

Hester: I don't remember if she was particularly strict with us or not. Do you?

Marianne: I think she was. More than I am with my kids.

Hester: That isn't difficult. You're a real pushover. And it was a different time, when parents were expected to be stricter.

Marianne: Funny, I can't think of anything specific now, although I remember her being strict.

Hester: Don't you remember the horrible brown lace-up shoes she made us wear? Or the sensible short haircuts – that's why I still insist on wearing my hair long. Yet she spoiled us too. The peeled and seeded grapes . . .

Marianne: When we were sick! That's the best, most comforting childhood memory I have of her. Her cool hand on my forehead, when something hurt.

Hester: We thought for a long time that she had healing powers in her hands. Did she?

Marianne: Do you still believe in the tooth fairy?

Hester: I don't know, I wish I could trust in Mam's magic the way I did then. Now that I have children of my own, I realise that being a mother forces you to become

magical – you start making up stories, you become a spin-
ner of tales. Your children expect it of you. But eventually
it starts to make you uncomfortable, because you're getting in deeper and deeper, and you realise that what
you're doing is telling them lies. What it boils down to is
you're trying to keep them from growing up.

Marianne: We did catch her out in the end, didn't we? The
magic sleeping potion that worked like a charm but that
turned out to be plain sugar dissolved in water. It took us
years to figure that one out. Didn't we feel cheated?

Hester: I think what I'm saying is that with Mam, I haven't
completely given up that need to believe. I usually assume
she has her reasons. For me she still has that magical side
to her. Her instincts are sometimes uncanny. And then
there's the dowsing, too. People consult her when they
need to dig a well for a new house. She's never failed to
find water.

Marianne: Even if it requires drilling through layers of solid
bedrock to get to it.

Hester: It's easy to be cynical. Like Daddy. Encouraging her,
but with a smirk, as if we know better.

Marianne: They had this double act going – Pap the straight
man, Mam the flake. She got teased about her use of
English, her compulsive house cleaning, her weak grasp of
geography. It was hard not to gang up with him, against her.

Hester: It's not fair. She's certainly as clever as he is, we've
always known that. She was the one to turn to if you
needed help with your maths homework, not Daddy. It
must have hurt.

Marianne: I think she set herself up. Deliberately. Has it
occurred to you that with Daddy, she was re-enacting her
role in her own family when she was a child, the easy tar-
get of family jokes? Think of the stories she'd tell us, of
how her father and older brothers used to put her down.

Her brothers used to regale the family and visitors with 'Edith-jokes' – stories with hilariously botched punch-lines, supposedly as told by Edith. And when she complained at dinner that she never got a chance to speak, her father would look at his watch and say sternly, 'OK, Edith has exactly one minute to say something important. Ready – GO!'

Hester: I suppose it seemed funny to us when we were young. Now I am horrified by it, because I relate it to my own feeling of having no voice, of not being able to hold my own in conversation. Which is why I resort to writing, where I am free to say what I like.

Marianne: The point, though, is that the picture she painted for us at the time, of her family in Holland before the war, was so glowing, so perfect. The wonderful family that we never knew, that was wiped out before we were born – it seemed so much more interesting to us than our own! All that fun, that warmth, the creativity, the endless celebrations marked with poems, songs and paintings, the musical evenings, the sailing expeditions with her brothers and their glamorous girlfriends, the skating parties in winter . . .

Hester: At the end of a day's skating, warming their freezing toes with steaming hot pea soup . . .

Marianne: How many years was it before we came to realise that they didn't actually take off their skates and dip their feet into vats of burning hot soup?

Hester: When I reread her diaries last year, one of the things that struck me was that the fun continued well after the German invasion, even after they were kicked out of school, right up to 1942, when news came that Jewish boys and girls were being rounded up for so-called 'work camps', and the decision was made that Edith and Jules should go into hiding.

Marianne: Luckily Guus, the oldest, was already out of harm's way in America.

Hester: Where they all could have been – *should* have been – if it hadn't been for the little problem of obtaining a visa for the grandmother who'd come to live with them when things got too hot in her native Heidelberg, but who still had a German passport. If it hadn't been for those US immigration quotas, they'd have been safe. They had their passage all booked and everything.

Marianne: They couldn't have left the old lady behind, could they?

Hester: So they all stayed, and they all died.

Marianne: Except Mam.

Hester: Mam, the survivor.

Marianne: What a contrast. The wonderful childhood up to the age of fourteen or fifteen, and the horror afterwards. No wonder her post-war family – the husband and three daughters – could never quite measure up.

Hester: I don't agree. I don't think she expected us to live up to her memories. I think she accepted us for what we were, and appreciated us for what we were. If anything, I think what she was doing was holding on to the good memories because they helped to offset the horrible ones, the ones that came later.

Marianne: Don't you see you're still doing it?

Hester: Doing what?

Marianne: Protecting her. Being protective.

Hester: We owe her that, at least.

Marianne: We owe her that – is that what it's about? Tit for tat? She gave us a happy childhood and we owe her for it? Or is it that we owe her for losing her own happy childhood?

Hester: I don't know, I just feel guilty for not doing enough for her, not showing my appreciation enough, not trying hard enough to make her happy. I get a pang when I read the soppy anniversary poems she wrote to her parents, or the loving letters they wrote to her, they were so openly . . .

Marianne: Sentimental?

Hester: To put it bluntly. It would be interesting to live in a time when sentimentality wasn't the great taboo it is to us.

Marianne: It's not that we can't appreciate it. It's just that we can't do it.

Hester: It's not your style, no. You're so good at hiding your feelings.

Marianne: Mam doesn't do it either – show her feelings, I mean. Not really.

Hester: She takes her cue from us, perhaps. She's very careful not to demand too much from us. It's a different world. She doesn't want to be out of step.

Marianne: Perhaps she taught herself to hide her feelings when she was in hiding. When she had to be so careful not to give herself away. And perhaps you could say I learned to hide my feelings from her.

Hester: How old would you say we were when we became aware of what happened to her during the war?

Marianne: We were certainly very young. Maybe four or five. Perhaps younger. We knew that Tante Tine wasn't our real grandmother, that our real grandparents had died in the war. The idea of the holocaust was very frightening. All those people who never came back.

Hester: I remember studying those pictures, in *Life* or *Paris Match*, of the cattle cars, the piles of bones, the gold fillings, the emaciated naked people. I had nightmares about the showers. The worst of it was that they had to take off all their clothes. I couldn't reconcile that with the pictures of our grandmother Hilde, the smiling lady with the heavy hair and the pretty blouses.

Marianne: I had nightmares about the lampshades made of human skin, and the soap . . .

Hester: And yet I had the sense that Mam was shielding us from the worst of it. We had to pry it out of her.

Marianne: Some of it was very vivid, though. The way she felt the night she went into hiding, when she had to unpick the yellow Star of David sewn to her clothes – terrified of leaving any telltale remnants of thread or lint, but so happy to be free . . .

Hester: The stories were sanitised for us, of course. That sort of detail was thrown in to conceal the unspeakable. After that night she never saw her family again.

Marianne: She didn't want us to feel sorry for her. She didn't want us to be afraid. She was always careful to assure us that the same thing would never happen to us.

Hester: Yet all my life, I've been waiting for it to happen. Waiting for the worst.

Marianne: Touch wood. Nothing really bad has happened to us. Yet.

Hester: Perhaps that's what makes me such an optimist. When something bad happens, I refuse to panic. Because I always think, 'This isn't the worst. It could be a lot worse.' So I always see the bright side of things.

Marianne: Like that saying we had tacked to the wall of our room, the one that used to make us laugh, how did it go . . .

Hester: *One day as I sat sad and lonely and without a friend, a voice came to me out of the gloom and said, 'Cheer up, things could be worse.' And so I cheered up, and sure enough, things got worse.*

Marianne: Even back then, in our childish self-centredness, we were aware that somehow she'd missed out. That she was hurt. We wanted to make it up to her.

Hester: Perhaps we felt we had to make up for her loss of

pride in who she was. And for the loss of her father, her grandmother, her favourite brother, her home, her friends. But most of all for the loss of her mother.

Marianne: Yes, that seemed the most terrifying thing of all. You couldn't kiss *that* better.

Hester: Strange – her mother was always such a part of our lives. Even though we never knew her. Not the white-haired granny she might have been had she lived, but Hilde, a woman the same age Mam was then, the same age we are now. It could have been any one of us – this middle-aged, middle-class mother whose life was cut short by a train ride to the gas chambers.

Marianne: Losing my mother was always my worst nightmare.

Hester: Was it? Mine too. I had this recurrent dream when we lived in Zandvoort – I must have been about six or seven years old – of Mam walking purposefully down the street, not looking back, and me running after her, crying, trying to get her to come back. I always woke up from it in a total sweat.

Marianne: Later, when we were teenagers, weren't we somehow aware of how lucky we were to have a mother? I'm sure we felt a need to go easy on her. We thought it was unfair to expect her to understand what this daughter–mother animosity was about – since she herself had been cheated of the chance to rebel against her own mother.

Hester: I don't think it was such a conscious thing on our part. But you're right, I do think we were holding back. We could have been a lot nastier to her.

Marianne: Or perhaps we simply don't remember how nasty we were.

Hester: Meanwhile Hilde was held up to us as a perfect, elegant, serene and wise creature. A being impossible ever to live up to, especially for poor gawky little Edith.

Marianne: I never thought of it that way before. I see it now: Hilde as the mother seen through Edith's eyes while she was still a child, before the realisation that one's parents are not perfect. Mam's relationship with her mother was frozen in time before she could see the flaws.

Hester: She couldn't rebel while she was in hiding with Tante Tine's family, either. When from one day to the next she stopped being Edith and became Nettie, the name on her forged papers. She needed to survive. Survival meant being the good, grateful, helpful girl in her new family, always mindful of the fact that these people who had taken her in were risking their own lives in order to save hers. Turning herself into the servant, the slave, the grateful underdog. When by rights she should have been slamming doors and rolling her eyes and being moody. Like us.

Marianne: And then there was the contrast between the warm, indulgent, artistic Jewish clan she had left behind and this Calvinistic Dutch family, morally righteous and immensely courageous, but cold and undemonstrative.

Hester: As a child I was always a little afraid of Tante Tine. She was like some revered but overly strict headmistress. No hugs, certainly no cuddles.

Marianne: Yet for all these years Mam has played the role of devoted daughter to the woman who saved her life.

Hester: Wouldn't you have done the same thing?

Marianne: Of course I would have. But I think Mam never feels she's done enough. Even after she had Tante Tine honoured in that tree-planting ceremony in Jerusalem, at Yad Vashem.

Hester: I think Tante Tine likes all the accolades, don't you? 'Righteous Gentile' – the name suits her.

Marianne: Yet she's always dourly protested that any 'decent' person would have done the same thing. That it was nothing. That she doesn't need any fuss.

Hester: You can never tell, with Tante Tine. I think that Tine has allowed herself to be defined by Mam's view of her as saviour and hero.

Marianne: But there is also genuine love there, I think. Despite the fact that Mam sometimes breaks out in hives before visiting her.

Hester: I think that it's Mam who needs this relationship most, who needs to pay tribute to her, to honour her for what she did.

Marianne: Yet we're all flying to Holland this summer to celebrate her 100th birthday, aren't we? So she's not the only one who needs to pay tribute.

Hester: I suppose not. But the rest of us are doing it mostly for Mam's sake. Shall I make a confession? I'm waiting for Tine to die, because when she does, I think it will make it easier for Mam to tell her story. There are still so many elements missing, so many things I feel she can't bring herself to talk about.

Marianne: But what I want to know is, why is it so important to us that she finish her story?

Hester: For posterity? So that the people who died will not be forgotten?

Marianne: That's not really the point. It seems to me that we have this great need to feel that she's done with it – to have it be a finished chapter in her life.

Hester: It's as if we are somehow responsible for her.

Marianne: We've *always* felt responsible. Strange – Mam didn't demand it of us, did she?

Hester: No, I think it was Daddy. He used to reprove us for giving her a hard time. He made us feel guilty for disturbing her when she was having one of her headaches. How I remember feeling abandoned, feeling guilty because *we* had nothing to complain about, compared to what *she* had to suffer.

212

Marianne: Oh yes, those headaches . . .

Hester: Do you remember how it felt when, a few years ago, Tante Tine casually let the bomb drop – 'Oh yes, it was when we got the news that your grandmother had been deported that Edith's headaches first started –'?

Marianne: Was I there? I certainly remember it, but perhaps you told me about it later. God, what a revelation! Everything suddenly fell into place. The dreaded headaches, our tiptoeing around the house, not knowing what to do with ourselves . . .

Hester: Of course we couldn't have associated the headaches with the war, at the time. Is it normal for children to resent their parents' infirmities? Or could it have been this buried link to the past that bothered us so much?

Marianne: I doubt it. I can't believe we could have been conscious of that. Yet I suppose in other ways the past was an important part of who she was.

Hester: Knowing what she had to go through as a child made her a hero to me. I was perversely proud of her – as if her suffering proved that she was better than other children's mothers.

Marianne: It's hard not to romanticise it, for a child.

Hester: Even for an adult! I still sometimes catch myself wallowing in the shivers-down-your-spine tragedy of it.

Marianne: And the adventure of it was appealing too. There were stories we just couldn't get enough of.

Hester: Even though I now realise the stories were doled out to us piecemeal. Never as a complete, chronological narrative. It was always bits and pieces. In a way it was unsatisfying, I wanted her to make sense of it for me, but I couldn't bring myself to ask, in case it got boring – or in case it became too sad – and I'd be obliged to stay and listen . . .

Marianne: It's true – we must have realised that her war was overwhelmingly tedious and dull most of the time, but the stories *we* wanted to hear were the ones that had action and suspense. Like the day she missed the train and found herself in a strange town after curfew with false identity papers and no place to hide, and she talked that vicar into letting her spend the night sitting in a chair in his parlour, so she wouldn't get picked up by the SS. Or when the German officer was billeted at their house, and Tante Tine decided that Mam should be the one to bring him his morning coffee so he wouldn't get suspect anything . . .

Hester: The wonderful childish revenge fantasies that this Nazi would fall head over heels in love with her, and find out, too late, that the object of his love was a Jew . . . !

Marianne: I realise there's also a certain amount of jealousy on our part. Nothing this exciting has ever happened to us. Do we allow her the romance of her past? It's difficult to acknowledge her central role in another story that doesn't involve us.

Hester: You're right. An ideal mother has no past – certainly nothing exotic – and lives only for her children.

Marianne: An ideal mother has no future, either. All those degrees, and yet she never really found the confidence to pursue a career.

Hester: She must have felt so lonely, after the war. That's why, when Papa gave her an ultimatum – marry me now, woman! – she caved in. Even though she was less than a year or so away from her doctorate.

Marianne: And then she had us. Twins.

Hester: A baby boom! I always felt there was some sort of poetic justice in the fact that the woman lying next to her in the maternity ward in Amsterdam was Miep Gies, Otto Frank's secretary, who had brought the Franks their food while they were in hiding. Miep was *their* Righteous Gentile . . .

Marianne: But, Anne Frank's diary hadn't been published yet, had it?

Hester: I think it had, just. Anyway, Miep and Mam exchanged stories, and when Miep's baby started having trouble nursing, Mam donated *her* surplus breastmilk . . .

Marianne: Breastmilk wasn't rationed, I suppose.

Hester: That story only really started to mean something to me after I'd had Anya. I was looking down at that busy little baby skull at my breast, and I started crying, thinking of Mam's milk for Miep's son, thinking about how perfectly life sometimes works itself out . . .

Marianne: Must have been your hormones. Did you ever tell Mam?

Hester: About being moved that way? Of course not.

Marianne: Anyway, the long and short of it is, Mam got herself knocked up, and it put an end to her dreams of becoming a psychologist.

Hester: It may have been more important to her just then to create a family to replace the one she'd lost, than to be Somebody With A Career.

Marianne: Afterwards, she did have regrets. She was always trying to make up for that unfinished degree by taking more exams, acquiring more qualifications. But she never had the confidence to take a job.

Hester: That's not true. She did have a few jobs. But they were half-hearted, part-time. I think it was partly because she has always had problems with the validity of her profession – I think she trusts her instincts more than the teachings she's supposed to follow as a psychologist.

Marianne: But it was also because she was never able to put her work first, before her role as a corporate wife.

Hester: And that's why, when it was our turn, it seemed so important to finish our studies and establish our careers, before getting married and having babies.

Marianne: We thought we should learn from her mistakes.

Hester: Do you think we did? Do you think our way was better?

Marianne: Probably not. I feel I'll never live up to her as a mother. Still, her inability to get somewhere in her career is one of the only things about Mam that we've ever allowed ourselves to criticise.

Hester: Well, I'm glad we found something to be critical of, at least. When I listen to my friends, one of the things that strikes me is that they can have such angry things to say about their mothers.

Marianne: They say that as you get older, you become afraid of turning into your own mother. Perhaps that's why they're angry.

Hester: Are you afraid of that?

Marianne: No. I don't think I'd mind – turning into Mam, I mean. She has dignity. She still sets standards for us to emulate. She still has better legs, too.

Hester: I agree, but now *you're* doing it.

Marianne: Doing what?

Hester: Being protective of her. Turning it into a tribute.

Marianne: Sorry.

Hester: See? We can't help ourselves.

Marianne: I think that's what our relationship with her is about – mutually protective – mutually appreciative. I don't think we ever truly rebelled against her, just as she never truly rebelled against her mother.

Hester: What about Jessica? She didn't hold back.

Marianne: Well, Jessica was born six years after us – more than ten years after the end of the war. She never had that sense of obligation. Our little sister definitely had a more classic adolescence. She's much more judgemental than we are.

Hester: You see? If anyone's going to write about Mam, it's got to be you or me. Imagine what Jessie would make of it!

Marianne: Jessica's reality is different from our reality. What do we know, anyway, about Mam? Where does *her* reality fit into all this?

Hester: Ask her.

Marianne: And make her put into a few words something that has taken me a lifetime to figure out? I know I probably wouldn't agree with her anyway. What's important is how *I* see her, I guess.

Hester: Or how *we* see her. But I do think you're getting somewhere. You really ought to try and write that piece.

Marianne: I still don't think I can do it by myself.

Hester: Nobody said you had to.

Lyd Sawyer

Shankara Angadi

SUCH A DISAPPOINTMENT

Patricia Angadi

How, I ask myself, does my mother manage, one way or
another, to edge her way into every book I write? Even when
I consider that I have deliberately left her out, friends or
relations see her presence. They smile at me knowingly and
say, 'I certainly recognised dear Auntie Clare in this one!'
And this when I have gone out of my way to describe a dear,
sweet, elderly idiot in a very fierce effort to get away from the
tall, stately beauty who sailed graciously through my childhood and adolescence.

When I started to write about my relationship with my
mother, I asked those who knew her what they remembered
best about her character, and I was fairly astounded at the
answers I got: 'Sweet and kind,' they said at once with the
sort of smile that conjured up a saintly Bellini madonna-

219

type, 'and so *witty*,' they added. Other epithets included generous, fun-loving, like Queen Mary (as against the Queen Mother), alarming, but overall 'a wonderful woman, quite awe-inspiring'.

This last was absolutely true: she inspired awe in everyone; partly, I think, on account of her looks. She was a good five foot ten and always wore heels that raised her to nearer six, her back was ramrod straight and she positively exuded dignity from every pore. But sweet? Kind? These were not the sort of adjectives with which I would have saddled my mother – not that she would ever have been consciously unkind, that was not in her nature. On the contrary, she constantly and genuinely emanated benevolence and philanthropy to all those who needed it, particularly charities and poor relations. I still have the medal she was awarded from the League of Mercy Charity operating in the First World War years, for which we had a collecting box, with a row of book matches (costing one penny) in front, placed strategically near the front door in our hall. There were the American Teas (now called Bring and Buy sales) which she organised at that time, and she took me on her philanthropic visits to children's hospitals at Christmas with bags of toys and goodies for the patients. On Christmas Day itself and all through the summer holidays our house was packed full of grateful, overawed relatives who were quite a bit poorer than we were.

So, without completely denying the label of 'kind and generous', I would think the description 'dutiful' might be a truer tag. I remember her once deciding to 'wear the mink' when she was going (in the Rolls) to open a church bazaar in Rotherhithe (a district neither she nor I had ever visited before) because 'they like you to dress up for that sort of thing'. I wonder if 'they' did. It's difficult to say whether the class-conscious snobbery of those times (the twenties) was resented then as bitterly as it would be today; perhaps it's just that the bazaar openers have changed from the Ladies Bountiful to Media Celebrities. The mink has probably become fake leopard, but the diamonds are bigger and the cars even more vulgar now than they were then.

It was not that my mother was born into the sort of life she was later to lead. She came from a middle-class, highly respectable family, with a father who started out as a poor but well-educated bank clerk in Hackney. She never admitted to being born in Hackney; I only discovered it from her birth certificate after she died. I heard stories of her childhood in Enfield where her greatly revered father had risen to the status of bank manager. She was the eldest, born in 1877, of three girls and a boy so, after a Victorian childhood, she emerged into marriage and motherhood as what one might term a typical Edwardian.

Even though I did not know her in that period, being born in 1914 when the whole era collapsed into the shambles and chaos of the Great War to end all wars, I still have the image of her as she must have appeared to my brothers and sister – set firmly in the Edwardian scene where Gibson Girl-type ladies seemed to be forever leaning laughingly forward in Walter Crane curves, their skirts swirling round their feet, and their luxuriously abundant hair piled, Beardsley fashion, high on their heads. A world where one was born into a class structure as rigid as the Hindu caste system and did not dream of moving out of it unless one was an anarchist agitator or my mother.

With a little bit of imagination, I have surmised that she was not content to linger with her sisters in the respectable confines of Enfield, but hankered after the bright lights and heady pleasures of London society. So she somehow became the favourite niece of her mother's ostracised eldest sister. This aunt had shocked her family by marrying a publican in the 1880s and was no longer received by them. However, the publican made good and, according to *The Times*, writing about him in 1907, 'associated himself with the brewing interest'. He was made an Alderman of the City of London in 1894, elected Sheriff in coronation year (1902) and was knighted, becoming Lord Mayor of London in 1907.

For some reason or other, my mother had been specially favoured by her aunt and uncle – though other nieces (and there were plenty of them) were ignored; she stayed with them in their house in Portland Place to 'do the Season', be presented at court and introduced into London society. I am not sure why she was singled out or how this approach was received by her parents: were they pleased at her good fortune? Proud or annoyed that she had been given this special treatment at the expense of her sisters and cousins? It is difficult to consider at this distance of time. I know that one of my aunts was, in fact, extremely jealous of her preferential treatment, though at pains to suppress the resentment she obviously felt.

My father's family also owned a house in Portland Place (as well as a castle in Scotland) which happened to be next door to my great uncle's; thus, my mother and father met in 1901, and married in Marylebone Parish Church in September 1902. My paternal grandfather had made a great deal of money in the 1860s by starting a paint and varnish firm, using the gums and oils brought to England from the East by his sea captain father during the 1840s and 50s; so Grandpa was one of the trade barons who became rich and powerful at the end of the nineteenth century and left his fortune to his two sons, my father and my uncle. Neither of them had much business sense, but managed to enjoy a very comfortable lifestyle on the proceeds right up to the end of the Second World War.

All this background perhaps goes some way to explain the

relationship between my mother and myself, because I was born at the beginning of the First World War when so much of the old style of living was beginning to be swept away for ever. Though my upbringing was fairly typically what was still known as 'upper middle class' (as distinct from upper class who were commonly – and I do mean 'commonly' in its class sense – known as 'the gentry'), I never really quite fitted in, however hard I tried. And I really did try, rather desperately, to join in with those other boarding-school types who came almost exclusively from Kensington, Scotland or Surrey, but I was probably much too boisterous and enthusiastic – especially when I became a débutante in 1932 – to make a success of it.

So I became a guilt-ridden Disappointment to my mother from the word go, and I still, in my eightieth year, feel distinctly guilty about it all.

My two brothers and one sister, who were all born between 1903 and 1908 into that historic Edwardian childhood which I missed out on, did all the right and conventional things during their youthful flings in the twenties and married conventionally suitable partners with conventionally suitable incomes and families. They didn't disappoint her (even my brothers' divorces only caused a medium blip in her approbation), whereas I, who, she often told me, had been the sweetest, most loving baby any mother could wish to have, had obviously grown up into the biggest disappointment of her life.

Of course she never actually said this; just turned away with tears in her eyes whenever I argued over something, or when I gave up learning bridge after she had arranged special lessons for me, or admired a picture or an individual she thought was unsuitable. After all, the things she did for me and said to me were *all for my own good*, and I was just being ungrateful and unkind to her by not appreciating this. And the dreadful thing was that this was perfectly true. When I look back now and see just how much I disappointed her later on, I can only feel quite aghast at the distress I caused her, and experience the guilt even more strongly than I did then.

Surprisingly, perhaps, I look back on my childhood as a gloriously golden period. In the usual way, all the summers were hot and sunny, life was one long list of pleasures and treats. Though I know that this was not true, and that my own make up is the sort that brushes unpleasant memories under the carpet and remembers only the good bits, I seem singularly to have failed to produce a balanced picture of my mother. If she was really as I have described her here and in my books, she must have been a dreadful mixture of snobbery, pained pique and malicious insensitivity – and I would be quite unjustified in my feeling of guilt; she would have deserved all she got and the label 'kind' would be a monstrous misnomer.

So what have I left out? Because my mother was no monster; she was an attractive, tolerant, much admired charmer with a good sense of fun, and this last asset is what I often tend to forget. She laughed a great deal – often quite helplessly – and tended to see the funny side of tense situations – as when Grandma's teeth fell out at the dinner table or when her own knickers fell down outside Debenham and Freebody's (then a very superior and expensive shop). After she had stepped out of them, the commissionaire, who was opening the car door for her, picked them up, folded them carefully, and hung them over her arm with a grave smile.

While being able to keep everyone on their toes in case they hurt her feelings, she was quite able to slide down the stairs on a tea tray with me and once, I believe, insisted on coming down one of the bob-sleigh runs in Switzerland. She took me to the Wembley British Empire Exhibition in 1924 and joined me on the helter skelter and water chute and chairoplanes at the fun fair after we had done the rounds of the various pavilions. She played a big part in instigating my love of music – admittedly in the high society way – by taking me to the opera at Covent Garden, as part of the London Season. We went in June (or was it July?) and sat, in our ermine and pearls, in the same seats in the third row of the stalls for every new performance. But we were both far more interested in the performance than in the celebrities who surrounded us, and that was more than could be said for the majority of the audience on those occasions.

Added to this pleasure we shared, I loved the way she took great delight in cheating, very obviously, at the games she played with me – beggar-my-neighbour, Ludo and croquet (especially croquet) whenever the opportunity arose. I think it was this sense of fun, and her ability to make witty comments under her breath on smart but boring occasions, that endeared her to everybody and kept the balance for me right through my life.

It was not, unfortunately, considered correct at that time to praise one's children because this was a form of conceit and would be bound to give them a false sense of their own importance, something to be avoided at all costs. One had to remember one's position in life and not make any attempt to pretend to be something one was not – like, for instance, an artist or an author or any sort of intellectual (heaven forbid), because this would be pretentious and silly; almost as silly and as unthinkable as suggesting one was one of the aristocracy. Harbouring any sort of ideas that might be considered as being above one's station could label one 'nouveau riche' and common. To consider oneself clever was even more unforgivable if you were female; men did not admire blue stockings and would never marry them.

So I (and many of my female friends of the same age group) grew up convinced we were plain, too fat (or too thin), and extremely silly. I had further proof of this by being nicknamed Jane by my mother and sister (Plain Jane of the Hills; I don't know who she was or where she came from, but she was often quoted) and Fat Pat by my brothers. Obviously a Tremendous Disappointment to my mother.

And all through this period of my life I was never able to talk to her about anything that really mattered. I could laugh with her, cuddle her, enjoy going about with her, but it was far too embarrassing to talk to her about personal things. Sex, of course, was something that did not exist in polite society and I grew up knowing nothing at all about it until I actually experienced it. From the age of four to middle age I was brought up by a governess who was recruited in 1918 and stayed for thirty-four years, by which time my eldest son was eight. She became not only my teacher but my most beloved companion and confidante but, although she was able to explain menstruation (after it had happened) and how the dog had puppies (but not how they got there), it was left to one of my boyfriends to provide me with Norman Haire's *Encyclopaedia of Sexual Knowledge.* To ask one's mother about such unmentionable things was unthinkable, and I think my governess probably knew little more than I did myself.

Mummy – she remained Mummy until I was well into my forties when the title became an embarrassment to me and was diffidently changed to Ma or Mamma – remained a distant, though affectionate and much loved, super-being who wafted through my early childhood. The stately, superbly garbed queen on whose bedroom door I knocked every morning at eight-fifteen to say 'good morning Mummy' (Daddy by this time was dressing in his dressing room) and watch for five minutes as she wound up her long hair or fastened the strings of pearls round her neck before I went to eat my Grapenuts in the nursery. The being who took me out in the car on special visits, read to me for half an hour every evening at six o'clock, occasionally bathed me (up to the age of six) as a special treat and always kissed me goodnight before she went down to dinner. A special being whom I loved and who kissed and cuddled me, sometimes played with me, occasionally – but not often – scolded me very gently and was always *there*, downstairs, while I got on with living and learning upstairs in the nursery with the governess. As I grew older (about seven) my governess and I were allowed to have lunch downstairs with the family, but breakfast and tea were always in the nursery and supper was biscuits and milk on a tray in my bedroom at seven o'clock. Changes to my life were never discussed with me before they were announced.

'You are going to the girls' school up the road in September, Tish darling,' said my mother when I was ten; so off I went, obediently and suitably excited. I was greatly relieved that my governess was allowed to stay on to take and fetch me, make and mend my clothes and to deal with me in the afternoons as I wasn't allowed to stay at school for lunch or afternoon prep and was only permitted to go to hockey or cricket with them twice a week.

And then in the summer of 1928, just before my fourteenth birthday when I was really deep into school life and enjoying it exuberantly, I was sent, unwilling and protesting rather feebly, to Prior's Field, a private boarding school in Surrey.

'I promise you, darling,' said my mother, 'if you don't like it you won't have to stay, I will fetch you home at once.'

So she was no ogre, my mother, merely following a tradition, but amending it a little because, I think, she had been shocked and upset at the grief shown by my brothers and sister who were sent away to board at seven and eight years old, as custom demanded. It might be essential for boys to be toughened up but by the time I was growing up, she had decided that girls could be treated differently. My sister never forgave me for getting preferential treatment.

I am not sure that I really merited the softer approach, because I would probably have delighted in the life wherever or whenever I had been sent. Being very adaptable, I was not in the least homesick and was boringly enthusiastic from day one about being part of the Angela Brazil environment I had read so much about.

Did I hurt her feelings by being so tiresomely steeped in school life? It never occurred to me at the time that I did, because I was equally enthusiastic about the holidays, even though I couldn't wait to get back to school when they were over. I did find, though, that my governess (who was still, surprisingly, kept on – possibly because she had nowhere else to go and could still deal with me in the holidays) had a more sympathetic ear where all the tedious accounts of lacrosse matches, school chums, and school plays were concerned. My mother's attention wandered before the journey, in the Rolls, from Waterloo Station to our Hampstead home, was accomplished, whereas my governess's 'Did you dear? That's nice,' while she poured the tea in the nursery or turned the handle of the old sewing machine, was much more satisfactory.

But I now think that I was probably already acting in a thoughtless, uncaring way, which was not, however, in any way rebellious – that was my sister's reaction; she felt that she was badly treated while I was spoilt and she took pains to make her feelings known. I never thought I was badly treated; memories of my childhood continue to remain golden and I was quite conscious that if I was ever upset it was bound to be my own fault. I did not have the perspicacity to imagine that my mother might be jealous of the affection I bore my governess, but I did notice that she was often rather unkind and sarcastic to her. I realised, by that time, that it was absolutely taboo to criticise or find fault with dear Mamma in any way, because it would upset her far too much. I was already very wary of hurting her feelings, which was such an easy thing to do.

Hardly a mention of my father! Sadly, this is how I remember him: always there, in the background, smoking the inevitable cigarette in the ivory holder with *The Times* crossword at the ready on one hand, a whisky and soda at the other. But never taking part; my mother ruled the roost, we were all her faithful subjects. She was, however, a benevolent dictator; never raised her voice to us, never ordered us to do anything, was never angry with us, just so convincingly distressed whenever we did anything of which she disapproved that we all remained in devoted awe, reacting in our own ineffectual ways – my father, by entering into a state of coughing and spluttering and cursing under his breath, my brothers by getting out of the way as quickly as possible, my sister by sulking and me by falling over backwards in my attempts not to arouse disapproval, but generally being too thick to notice when I was responsible for doing so.

When the big crunch came, I became the greatest cause of distress that was possible for my mother to face. At the beginning of the Second World War, I decided to marry a penniless, left-wing Indian. I was so won over by his invincible arguments of the rightness of the deed that I rode roughshod over the pleadings and the tears and the distress, sailing enthusiastically into the next period of my life.

Of course we were right and she was wrong; I gained all the confidence and assurance I had been denied until then, and found myself capable of achieving things I would never have dreamed of attempting before. But my mother could not imagine that this would happen and kept telling me that she was only thinking of my happiness in her attempts to make me give up the whole distressful idea. I knew at the time that this was not actually true, though I am sure she thought it was: it was the terrible disgrace to her and to the whole family that was at the back of the resistance. *I had married a black*!

Nevertheless, the guilt I now feel is because of the unforgivable way I did ride roughshod, gaily taking for granted the fact that we should naturally live with my parents after the war because we had no money to do anything else. I ignored what she felt was the disgrace and humiliation of having to admit to her friends that her daughter had married what was then known as a Native. 'Black' was far too coarse a word for her to use. Some years before this, one of my school friends had married a Siamese prince which I thought very impressive, but all my mother could say was, 'What a disaster – her poor, poor mother must be heart-broken.' I was astounded at the time.

It is only now that I can feel sympathy, however wrong she might have been in her ideas, and guilty that I took for granted as my right the bed, board, support and affection which she continued to provide. And I just love the way she gradually came to accept the situation through her devotion to our children, even to the extent of forgetting herself once some eight years later by telling her friends, 'They've just come back from the sea and look bursting with health – they're as brown as berries!'

The sad thing is that I could never have written this, or any of my novels, if my mother had still been alive; she would have taken personally everything that had the slightest hint of any reference to herself and been mortally offended. She would never have got over it and would have remained a martyr for the rest of her days.

I wonder how many other daughters feel the same. I like

to think that my own daughter would have no difficulty in writing about me because I could argue and perhaps feel slightly hurt at what she might say, but I would not bite my lip and shed a tear in private. I think we would, I *hope* we would, discuss the whole thing with a great deal of laughter and argument and feel closer at the end of it, because I would probably be convinced that she was perfectly right and start feeling guilty all over again.

So perhaps it's just me and my guilt-ridden generation, and perhaps I don't really have to feel guilty at all – except for feeling guilty.

BIOGRAPHIES

PATRICIA ANGADI was born in London in 1914. After an upbringing that included a presentation at court, she abandoned her conservative English lifestyle to marry Ayana Angadi, an Indian writer and lecturer, Trotskyite and intellectual. Together they founded the Asian Music Circle in the late 1940s, organising an almost continuous programme of concerts for many years. Throughout this time Patricia was establishing herself as a talented portrait painter. At the age of fifty she took a teacher training course and subsequently taught in a primary school for thirteen years. On retiring, she started to write full time, and is the author of seven published novels, amongst them *The Governess, The Done Thing* and, most recently, *My Mother Said*. She lives in north London.

NINA BAWDEN was born in London and educated at Ilford County High School for Girls and Somerville College, Oxford. She is the author of twenty-one adult novels, including *Circles of Deceit* which was short-listed for the Booker Prize, and seventeen novels for children, including *Carrie's War* and *The Peppermint Pig* which won the Guardian Prize for Children's Literature. She has written a memoir *In My Own Time: Almost an Autobiography*. For ten years she served as a magistrate, both in her local court and in the Crown Court. She has also sat on the councils of various literary bodies, including the Royal Society of Literature, PEN, the Society of Authors, and the ALCS, and is the President of the of Women Writers and Journalists. She is married to Austen Kark, formerly Managing Director of the External Services of the BBC. They live in London and Greece.

MARGARET BUSBY was born in Ghana, West Africa (of African and Caribbean parentage), and was educated in England. On graduating from London University she co-founded the publishers Allison and Busby of which she was Editorial Director for twenty years (1967–87). From 1987 to 1990 she was the Editorial Director of Earthscan Publications. Since then she has worked in a freelance capacity as a writer, journalist, editor and consultant for many literary ventures, has served as a judge for several national competitions and has undertaken a wide variety of radio and television work. She has written articles and reviews for numerous publications, and was a contributor to the anthology *Colours of a New Day: Writing for South Africa*. She is the editor of *Daughters of Africa: An International Anthology of Writing by Women of African Descent from the Ancient Egyptian to the Present* (1992). She lives in London.

GABRIELLE DONNELLY was born in 1952 in Muswell Hill, London. She was educated at St Angela's Providence Convent Grammar School and Royal Holloway College, London University. She has been a journalist since 1974. In 1980, she moved to Los Angeles, where she has lived ever since, reporting on show business for British magazines, writing, and lecturing. She is the author of four novels, *Holy Mother, Faulty Ground, All Done with Mirrors* and *The Black and White Girl*, and has also co-authored, with Julia Braun Kessler, under the pen name of Julia Barrett, *Presumption*, a sequel to Jane Austen's *Pride and Prejudice*. She regards her decision to move to California as one of the best she ever made. 'A problem our whole family has faced,' she says, 'is that, nationally speaking, we're neither really English, nor properly Irish – foreigners in both camps. Most Americans are within a hundred years of being immigrants themselves, so over here, I fit right in.'

JOANNA GOLDSWORTHY (*Editor*) was born in 1941 in Redhill, Surrey, the eldest of five children. When she was ten, the family emigrated to Africa – South Africa, Southern Rhodesia, Kenya and Tanganyika – where she went to school and lived until she was twenty-three. Leaving Dar-es-Salaam – and her first husband whom she married when she was twenty – she went to work in London as the publisher Victor Gollancz's secretary. After his death she became first Editorial Director of the Gollancz children's books list, then Publishing Director of the adult list. She now works both as a freelance editor and as Associate Editor of Doubleday, London. She is the Editor of *A Certain Age: Reflections on the Menopause* (Virago, 1993).

MIRA HAMERMESH was born in Lodz, Poland. Her education was affected by the vagaries of the Second World War and her experiences as a refugee. In 1942 she was one of a group of Jewish children who found safety in Palestine. Her passion for painting began in childhood and at the age of sixteen she had an exhibition in Jerusalem, organised by the British Council. At the end of the war, an art scholarship and family connections took her to London where she studied at the Slade School of Fine Arts. In 1960 she was awarded a scholarship to study at the celebrated Polish Film School in Lodz. As a filmmaker, she has won many international awards, amongst them the Prix Italia and the Royal Television Award. An active feminist, she lives in London, not far from her son and two grandchildren.

GEORGINA HAMMICK was born in Hampshire and educated in Kenya and England. She studied drawing at the Académie Julian in Paris and then went to the Salisbury School of Art. She taught English and art before marrying Charles Hammick; together they started the first Hammick's bookshop in Farnham in 1968. She has published poems and for many years took part in the Poetry Society's Poet in Schools scheme. She is on the executive of English PEN and has served on the literature panels of the Greater London Arts Association and Southern Arts. She is the author of two collections of short stories, *People for Lunch* (1987) and *Spoilt* (1992) and is the editor of *The Virago Book of Love and Loss* (1992). She has three grown-up children and lives in Wiltshire.

ZOË HELLER was born in London in 1965. She has one brother, Bruno, and two sisters, Emily and Lucy. She studied at Oxford University and Columbia University in New York. She is a feature writer for *The Independent on Sunday* and *The New Yorker*. She currently lives in New York.

YASMIN KUREISHI was born in 1958 in Bromley, Kent. For nine years she studied dance at Bush Davies ballet school and the Weguelin School of Russian Ballet. She then worked as an office junior and later a telex operator, took her 'O' and 'A' levels, and went to the Polytechnic of North London where she read philosophy. She has written for the newspaper *Dawn* in Pakistan and for *Inside Asia* magazine. She was also a contributor and collective member of *Spare Rib*. After her son was born in 1989, she took a postgraduate Certificate in Education at Goldsmiths College, and now works as a full-time teacher in a primary school. She writes short stories and has completed a stage play..

ANNE LEATON was born and educated in Texas, and after going to Berlin on a Fulbright scholarship, lived in Europe, Africa and the Middle East for twenty years, returning to the United States in the 1970s. She has taught from time to time in universities, and has done, besides, a host of miscellaneous jobs (bond department of a bank in San Francisco, reducing salon in New Haven, antiquarian bookstore in New York). She has written poems, short stories (her first published short story was in the Transatlantic Review), and radio plays, and is the author of several novels including *Good Friends, Just* and *Mayakovsky, My Love.* Another novel is in the works. She now lives in Fort Worth, Texas.

JEANINE McMULLEN was born in Sydney, Australia, and spent a turbulent childhood wandering around New South Wales with her vivid and unconventional mother. She trained as a teacher and, after a few years of highly unorthodox classroom experiences, came to England to study at the Laban Art of Movement Centre. For two years she taught dance and drama in the East End of London but finally achieved her childhood ambition to be 'a lady on the radio', and subsequently worked for the BBC on the *Today* programme, *You and Yours* and innumerable features and documentaries. In the early seventies she bought a small-holding in Wales which later became the background for her successful programme *A Small Country Living* which ran for eleven years. She is the author of three books about her life in Wales, which she shared with her mother.

JULIA NEUBERGER was born in London in 1950 and educated at South Hampstead High School, Newnham College, Cambridge and Leo Baeck College, London. She became a rabbi in 1977 and served the South London Liberal

Synagogue for twelve years before going to the King's Fund Institute to work on research ethics committees in the United Kingdom. She was then a fellow at Harvard Medical School, and became Chairman of Camden and Islington Community Health Services NHS Trust in 1993. She serves on a number of councils and policy review boards and is the elected Chancellor of the University of Ulster. She broadcasts frequently and is the author of several books on women, on Judaism, on healthcare ethics and on caring for dying people. She is married to Anthony Neuberger, has two teenage children and lives in London.

SOPHIE PARKIN was born in London in 1961 to art dealer Michael Parkin and writer Molly Parkin. After getting a degree in fine art at St Martin's, Leeds and Maidstone Schools of Art, she ran night clubs in London, Hong Kong and Australia. She painted figurative oils from 1980 to 1992, with seven one-person shows in London and Spain, was art critic for *City* magazine, and was a performing poet. She is currently assistant agony aunt for *TV Quick* magazine, culinary expert at the Academy Club in Soho, and has written her first novel, *All Grown Up*. The brilliant survivor of an alcoholic childhood, she is the single mother of Paris and Carson Parkin-Fairley.

CAROLE STONE was born in 1942 in Maidstone, Kent. She joined the BBC at twenty-one as a junior secretary and worked her way via local and regional radio to become the producer of Radio 4's *Any Questions?* series, which she ran for ten years before leaving the BBC in 1990. She went on to devise and present *Mother of Mine* for BBC morning television in which she interviewed celebrities and their mothers. She was then a reporter on BBC television's right-to-reply programme, *Bite Back*. Carole is now a media consultant and has a small independent television company, Lindley Stone, which she set up with her partner, the current affairs reporter Richard Lindley. She writes for various magazines and newspapers and lives in London.

HESTER and MARIANNE VELMANS were born twenty minutes apart in Amsterdam in 1950. Their early years were spent shuttling back and forth between New York, Paris, Amsterdam (where their younger sister Jessica was also born), The Hague and finally Geneva, where they lived for ten years and attended the International School. Then came university in England – Hester at King's College, London and Marianne at the University of Sussex. After that, they shared a flat in London for several years, Hester working in magazine publishing and television news, and Marianne in book publishing. It was marriage that eventually separated them: Hester now lives near New York with her American husband and two children. She is the author of a novel and a children's book. Marianne remained in London, where she lives with her English husband and *her* two children. She is Publishing Director of the Doubleday imprint at Transworld Publishers, and is the co-author of a book about working mothers.

HARRIET WALTER was born and spent most of her childhood in London. She attended various schools, the most formative of which was Cranbourne Chase near Salisbury. After three years training at LAMDA, she spent her first six working years doing community and political theatre and concentrating on new writing with companies like 7:84, Joint Stock and Paines Plough. A somewhat late starter in 'legitimate' theatre, she crammed the eighties with work at the Royal Court and the Royal Shakespeare Company. Her TV appearances include *The Price*, Harriet Vane in *The Dorothy*

Sayers Mysteries and *The Men's Room*; her films *The Good Father* and Louis Malle's *Milou en Mai*; and her recent theatre includes *Three Birds Alighting on a Field* (Royal Court and New York), *Arcadia* and *The Children's Hour* (National Theatre).

Also of interest from Virago

FATHERS
Reflections By Daughters

Edited by Ursula Owen

'Moving and honest . . . extraordinarily searching
and articulate' – *Times Educational Supplement*

'This splendid book . . . will confirm, enlighten,
console and, yes, inspire' – *Women's Review of Books*

Of all the shaping human relationships, the one between
father and daughter is the least written about, especially
from the daughter's point of view. This book is a collage
of memoirs and polemic, stories and poems, describing
experiences which range from the most intense loyalty
and love to the dark and painful areas of paternal
tyranny and incest. Every daughter and every father will
recognise something of their story here: some will
realise, perhaps for the first time, just how deeply this
bond has affected their lives. For these writers, whose
ages range from thirteen to sixty, have produced
fascinating and sometimes shocking insights into what is
probably the most unresolved relationship of them all.

Contributors include Angela Carter, Elaine Feinstein,
Doris Lessing, Sara Maitland, Alice Munro, Grace Paley,
Adrienne Rich, Michèle Roberts, Sheila Rowbotham,
Alice Walker and many more.

BETWEEN OURSELVES
Letters between Mothers and Daughters

Edited by Karen Payne

**'One of the strongest contributions yet to the
honouring and understanding of the relationship
between mothers and daughters'** – *Tillie Olsen*

An extraordinary collection of letters between mothers
and daughters, from 1750 to the present, *Between
Ourselves* reveals the ways in which women through the
ages have struggled to break free of constraints and defy
society. With fascinating insights into the lives of the
famous – Anne Sexton, Florence Nightingale, Vera
Brittain, Queen Victoria and Sylvia Plath – as well as
the unknown – housewives, construction workers,
secretaries, political activists, teachers and scientists –
this absorbing and intense collection displays the vitality
and restless, questioning spirit of all women.

SUCH DEVOTED SISTERS
An Anthology of Stories

Edited by Shena Mackay

'That most rare of volumes, a sisterly literary companion' – *Irish Times*

Never were there such devoted sisters . . . or so the song would have it. Though some may be inseparable, for others the relationship arouses intense, tangled emotions. Louisa May Alcott, Elizabeth Gaskell, Georgina Hammick, Elizabeth Jolley, Katherine Mansfield and Edna O'Brien are among the prestigious writers who unravel this intricate bond.

Stories that reveal unbreakable allegiances and private codes are counterpointed by those of sisters pitched against one another in battles for parental affection or sibling supremacy. Rivalry, companionship, love and dislike feature in a collection that exposes the innermost secrets of family life. As delightful, surprising – and sometimes disturbing – as the ties they explore, these stories are essential reading.